iPad® for Seniors

Studio Visual Steps

iPad®
for Seniors

Quickly start working with the user-friendly iPad

www.visualsteps.com

This book has been written using the Visual Steps™ method.
Cover design by Studio Willemien Haagsma bNO

© 2012 Visual Steps
With the assistance of Yvette Huijsman
Edited by Jolanda Ligthart, Rilana Groot and Mara Kok
Translated by Irene Venditti, *i-write* translation services and Chris Hollingsworth, *1ˢᵗ Resources*.

Fourth printing: October 2012
ISBN 978 90 5905 108 9

Resources used: A number of definitions and explanations of computer terminology are taken over from the *iPad User Guide.*

Do you have questions or suggestions?
E-mail: info@visualsteps.com

Would you like more information?
www.visualsteps.com

Website for this book:
www.visualsteps.com/ipad
Here you can register your book.

Subscribe to the free Visual Steps Newsletter:
www.visualsteps.com/newsletter

Table of Contents

Mac for SENIORS

*LEARN
STEP BY STEP
HOW TO WORK
WITH MAC OS X*

The Macintosh line of desktop computers and laptops from Apple has enjoyed enormous popularity in recent years amongst a steadily growing group of users. Have you recently found your way to Apple's user-friendly operating system but are still unsure how to perform basic tasks? This book will show you step by step how to work with a Mac.

You will learn how to use basic features, such as accessing the Internet, using e-mail and organizing files and folders. You will also get acquainted with some of the handy tools and Apps included on the Mac that make it easy to work with photos, video and music. Finally, you will learn how to change the look and feel of your Mac interface and learn how to set preferences to make it even easier to work on your Mac. This practical book, written using the well-known step by step method from Visual Steps, is all you need to feel comfortable with your Mac!

Author: Studio Visual Steps
ISBN 978 90 5905 008 2
Book type: Paperback, full color
Nr of pages: 296 pages
Accompanying website:
www.visualsteps.com/mac

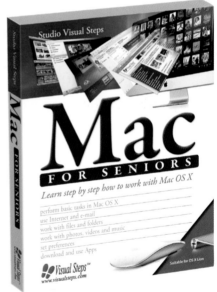

You will learn how to:
- perform basic tasks in Mac OS X
- use Internet and e-mail
- work with files and folders
- work with photos, videos and music
- set preferences
- download and use apps

Suitable for:
OS X Mountain Lion and Lion

Foreword

The iPad is an extremely user-friendly, portable multimedia device with countless possibilities. This device is ideal for all sorts of purposes, for instance surfing the Internet, sending and receiving e-mails, taking notes, or keeping a diary.

But this useful device has much more to offer. There are a number of standard apps (programs) available for working with photos, video, and music. You can even look up addresses and well-known places around the world, with *Maps*.
Also, you can go to the *App Store* and download numerous free and paid apps and games. What about recipes, horoscopes, fitness exercises, and stories to read aloud? You name it, and there will be some useful app to be got.

In this book you will get acquainted with the main functions and options of the iPad, step by step and in at your own pace.

You can work through this useful book independently, and at your own pace. Put the book next to your iPad and execute all the operations, step by step. The clear instructions and multitude of screenshots will tell you exactly what to do.
This is the quickest way of learning to use the iPad. Simply by doing it. A whole new world will appear!

I wish you lots of fun in working with the iPad!

Yvette Huijsman
Studio Visual Steps

PS After you have worked through this book, you will know how to send an e-mail. We welcome your comments and suggestions. Our e-mail address is:
info@visualsteps.com

Visual Steps Newsletter

All Visual Steps books follow the same methodology: clear and concise step-by-step instructions with screen shots to demonstrate each task. A complete list of all our books can be found on our website **www.visualsteps.com** You can also sign up to receive our **free Visual Steps Newsletter**.

In this Newsletter you will receive periodic information by e-mail regarding:
- the latest titles and previously released books;
- special offers, supplemental chapters, tips and free informative booklets.
Also, our Newsletter subscribers may download any of the documents listed on the web pages **www.visualsteps.com/info_downloads**

When you subscribe to our Newsletter you can be assured that we will never use your e-mail address for any purpose other than sending you the information as previously described. We will not share this address with any third-party. Each Newsletter also contains a one-click link to unsubscribe.

Introduction to Visual Steps™

The Visual Steps handbooks and manuals are the best instructional materials available for learning how to work with the iPad and other computers. Nowhere else can you find better support for getting to know an iPad, the Internet, *Windows*, *Mac* and computer programs.

Properties of the Visual Steps books:
- **Comprehensible contents**
  Addresses the needs of the beginner or intermediate computer user for a manual written in simple, straight-forward English.
- **Clear structure**
  Precise, easy to follow instructions. The material is broken down into small enough segments to allow for easy absorption.
- **Screenshots of every step**
  Quickly compare what you see on your screen with the screen shots in the book. Pointers and tips guide you when new windows are opened so you always know what to do next.
- **Get started right away**
  All you have to do is turn on your computer, place the book next to your device and execute the operations on your own iPad.
- **Layout**
  The text is printed in a large size font. Even if you put the book next to your iPad, this font will be clearly legible.

In short, I believe these manuals will be excellent guides for you.

dr. H. van der Meij
Faculty of Applied Education, Department of Instruction Technology, University of Twente, the Netherlands

What You Will Need

To be able to work through this book, you will need a number of things:

An iPad 2, the new iPad (third generation), the fourth generation iPad or iPad Mini with Wi-Fi or 3G/4G.

Probably, this book can also be used for a later edition of the iPad. For more information, see the webpage **www.visualsteps.com/ipad**

A computer or a notebook computer with the *iTunes* program installed. In *Appendix B Download and Install iTunes* you can read how to install *iTunes*.

If you do not own a computer or notebook, you may be able to execute these operations on the computer of a friend or family member.

You will need a printer with the Airprint option for the exercises about printing. You do not have a printer? Then you can skip the printing exercises.

At the time this book was written, there were only a few HP printers on the market that supported printing via the iPad.

How to Use This Book

This book has been written using the Visual Steps™ method. The method is simple: you put the book next to your iPad and execute all the tasks step by step, directly on your iPad. Because of the clear instructions and the multitude of screenshots, you will know exactly what to do. By executing all the tasks at once, you will learn how to use the iPad in the quickest possible way.
In this Visual Steps™ book, you will see various icons. This is what they mean:

Techniques
These icons indicate an action to be carried out:

 The index finger indicates you need to do something on the iPad's screen, for instance, tap something, or type a text.

The keyboard icon means you should type something on the keyboard of your iPad or your computer.

 The mouse icon means you should do something on your computer with the mouse.

 The hand icon means you should do something else, for example rotate the iPad or switch it off. The hand will also be used for a series of operations which you have learned at an earlier stage.

Apart from these operations, in some parts of this book extra assistance is provided to help you successfully work through this book.

Help
These icons indicate that extra help is available:

 The arrow icon warns you about something.

 The bandage icon will help you if something has gone wrong.

 The hand icon is also used for the exercises. These exercises at the back of each chapter will help you repeat the operations independently.

 Have you forgotten how to do something? The number next to the footsteps tells you where to look it up at the end of the book in the appendix *How Do I Do That Again?*

In separate boxes you will find general information or tips concerning the iPad.

Extra information
Information boxes are denoted by these icons:

 The book icon gives you extra background information that you can read at your convenience. This extra information is not necessary for working through the book.

 The light bulb icon indicates an extra tip for using the iPad.

Website

This book has its own: **www.visualsteps.com/ipad**
Visit this website regularly and check if there are any recent updates or additions to this book, or possible errata.

Test Your Knowledge

After you have worked through this book, you can test your knowledge online, at the **www.ccforseniors.com** website.

By answering a number of multiple choice questions you will be able to test your knowledge of the iPad. After you have finished the test, your *Computer Certificate* will be sent to the e-mail address you have entered.
Participating in the test is **free of charge**. The computer certificate website is a free Visual Steps service.

For Teachers

The Visual Steps books have been written as self-study guides for individual use. Although these books are also well suited for use in a group or a classroom setting. For this purpose, some of our books come with a free teacher's manual. You can download the available teacher's manuals and additional materials at:
www.visualsteps.com/instructor
After you have registered at this website, you can use this service for free.

The Screen shots

The screen shots in this book indicate which button, file or hyperlink you need to click on your computer or iPad screen. In the instruction text (in **bold** letters) you will see a small image of the item you need to click. The black line will point you to the right place on your screen.
The small screen shots that are printed in this book are not meant to be completely legible all the time. This is not necessary, as you will see these images on your own iPad screen in real size and fully legible.

Here you see an example of such an instruction text and a screenshot of the item you need to click. The black line indicates where to find this item on your own screen:

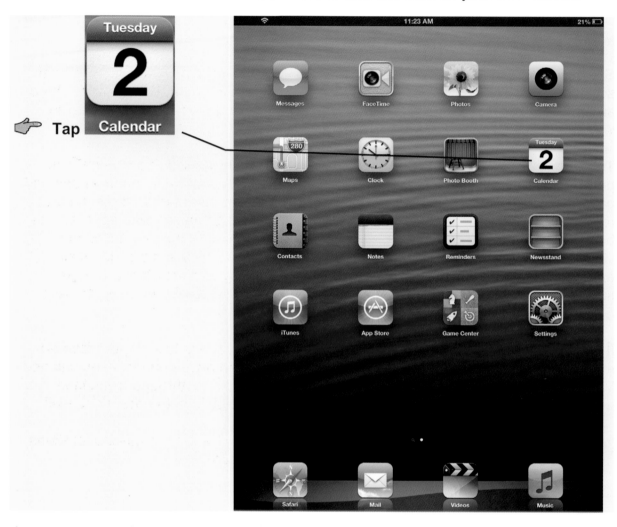

In some cases, the screen shot only displays part of the screen. Below you see an example of this:

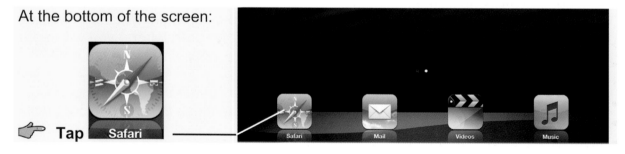

We would like to emphasize that we **do not intend you** to read the information in all of the screenshots in this book. Always use the screenshots in combination with the display on your iPad screen.

1. The iPad

Since the introduction of the first iPad in January 2010, millions of iPads have been sold. The iPad has now become the best selling *tablet* computer in the world. There are several editions of the iPad available today, but each iPad works in the same way.

The popularity of the iPad is not so surprising if you consider how lightweight and portable the iPad is and how easy it is to use. It has many of the same functions and capabilities of a regular computer. Not only can you surf the Internet and send and receive e-mails, you can also maintain a calendar, play games or read your favorite book, newspaper or magazine. You can also take pictures or make a movie and view or share them easily with others. You can do all this by using the so-called *apps*, the programs that are installed on the iPad. Along with the standard apps supplied on your iPad, you can easily add more (free and paid) by visiting the *App Store*, the web shop with all the apps.

If you connect your iPad to the computer, you can use *iTunes* to load your favorite music, movies, tv series and podcasts onto it. When you have done this you can use the iPad wherever you want. You can connect to the Internet through a wireless network (Wi-Fi) and with the 3G or 4G version, to the mobile data network as well.

In this chapter you will get to know your iPad and you will learn the basic operations necessary to operate the iPad and the onscreen keyboard.

In this chapter you will learn about:

- turning the iPad on or waking it up from Sleep Mode;
- initial setup;
- connecting the iPad to the computer;
- configuring the iPad in *iTunes*;
- safely disconnecting the iPad;
- the most important components of your iPad;
- updating the iPad;
- the basic operations for the iPad;
- using the onscreen keyboard;
- connecting to the Internet via a wireless network (Wi-Fi);
- connecting to the Internet via the mobile data network;
- putting the iPad into Sleep Mode or turning it off.

1.1 Turning the iPad on or Waking it up from Sleep Mode

The iPad can be turned off or locked. If your iPad is turned off, here is how you turn it on:

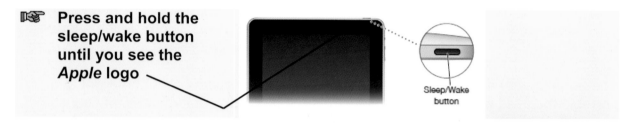

☞ **Press and hold the sleep/wake button until you see the *Apple* logo**

Now the iPad will power up:

Next, you will see the lock screen.

The iPad may also be locked. This is called Sleep Mode. If your iPad is locked, you can unlock it in the following way:

☞ **Press the Home button**

Now you will see the locked screen of the iPad. Here is how you unlock the iPad:

☞ **Drag the slider to the right**

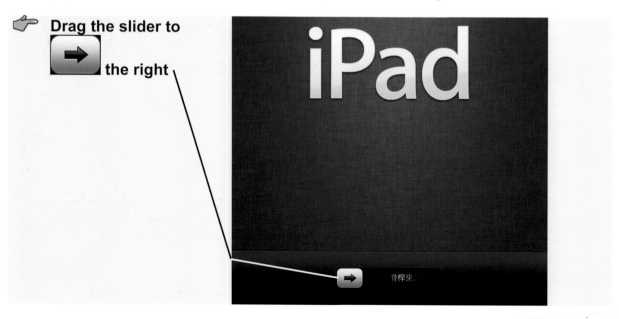

1.2 Initial Set Up of the iPad

When you start up your iPad for the very first time you will see a few screens where you are asked to enter some basic information. If you have already used your iPad before, you can skip this section and go to page 26. The first thing to do is set the language and country settings for your iPad:

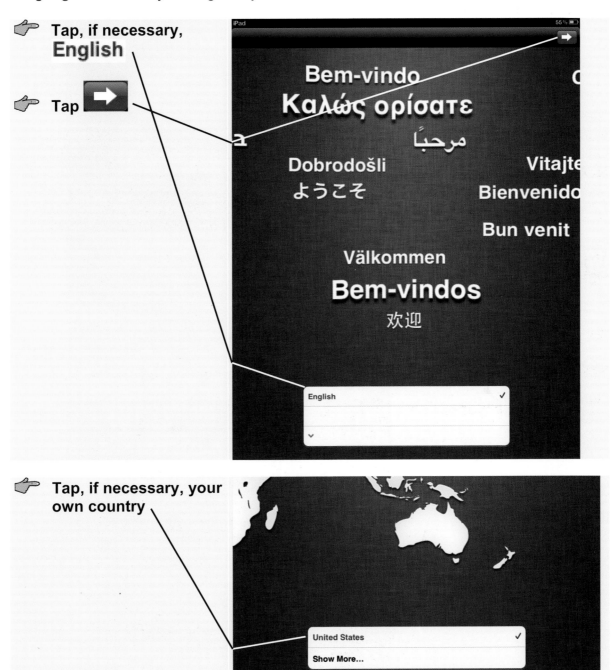

👉 **Tap, if necessary,**
English

👉 **Tap** ➡️

👉 **Tap, if necessary, your**
own country

In the top of this screen:

☞ **Tap**

In the next screen, you will be asked to choose your Wi-Fi network.

☞ **Tap your network** ———

⌨ **Type the password** ——

Does your password contain capital letters or numbers? Go to page 48 to read how to type them

☞ **Tap** Join

When the iPad is connected to the network:

☞ **Tap** Next

Note: if you have a micro SIM card for your 3G/4G data plan, you may not see this screen.

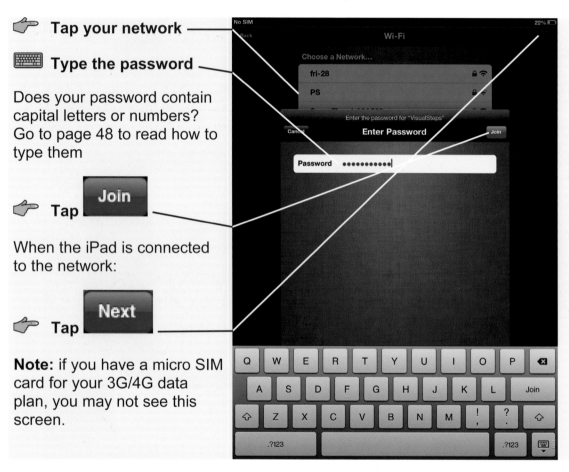

 Help! I don't have Wi-Fi.
If you do not have Wi-Fi available or prefer not to use it, then you will need to connect the iPad to *iTunes* on your computer in order to continue. You can use the USB cable that came with the packaging to do this.

In the Wi-Fi Networks screen:

☞ **Tap** 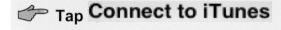 **Connect to iTunes**

- Continue on the next page -

A small window will appear:

☞ Tap **Continue**

🖝 Continue further with the steps in section *1.3 Connecting the iPad to the Computer*

You will be asked if you want to turn on Location Services. Location Services lets the iPad physically locate you using its built-in GPS. You can decide later on if you want to keep this service turned on or off. To turn Location Services on:

☞ Tap **Enable Location Services**

☞ Tap **Next**

You will probably see this screen:

In this example, a new iPad is being set up for the first time

☞ **Tap, if necessary,**
Set Up as New iPad

☞ **Tap** Next

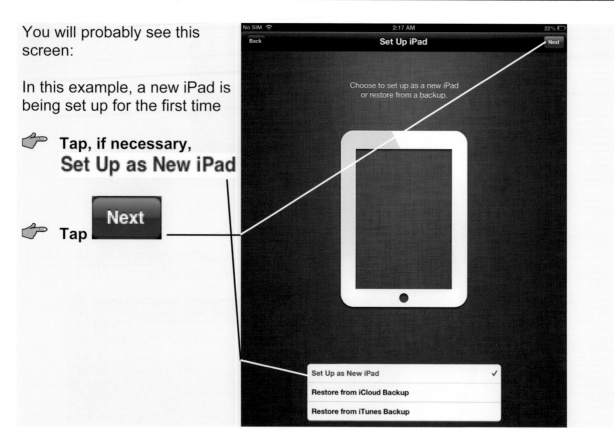

You will be asked if you want to log in with your *Apple ID*, or if you want to create a new one. You don't need to do either of these right now.

☞ **Tap** Skip This Step

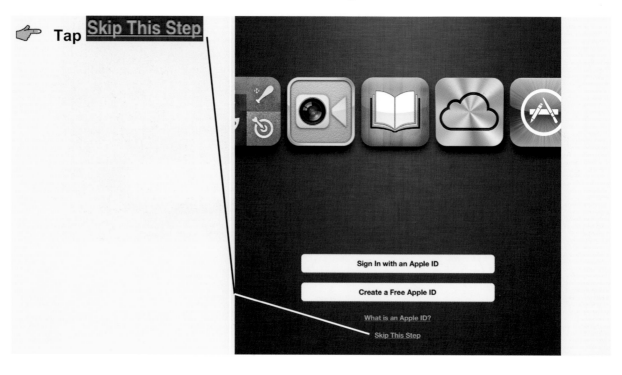

This window asks if you are sure you want to skip this step.

Tap **Skip**

The next screen displays Apple's Terms and Conditions. You must agree to these terms in order to be able to work with your iPad.

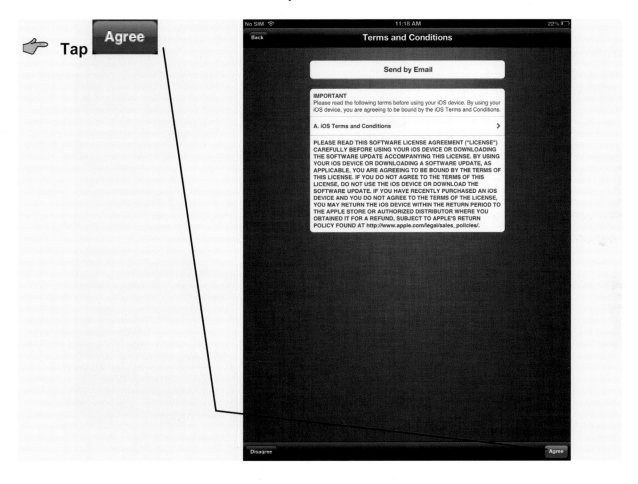

Tap **Agree**

In this small window you are asked to confirm:

☞ **Tap** Agree

The iPad asks if you want to use the dictation option:

☞ Tap **Use Siri**

If you don't want to use the dictation option you need to tap

Don't Use Siri .

☞ **Tap** Next

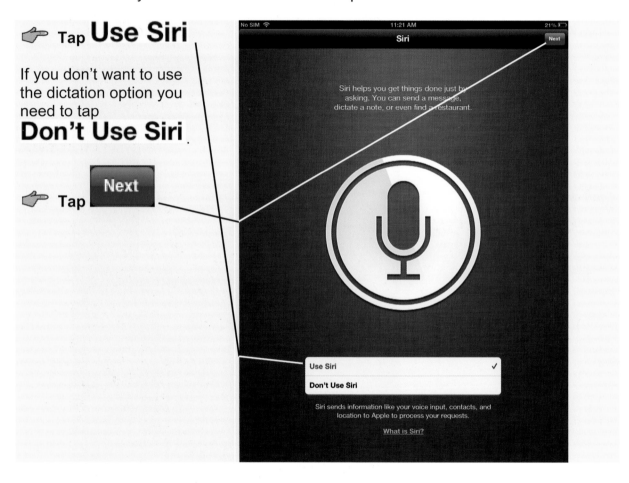

In the next window you are asked if you want to assist Apple with the improvement of their products by sending them diagnostic and usage data. You can skip this step for now.

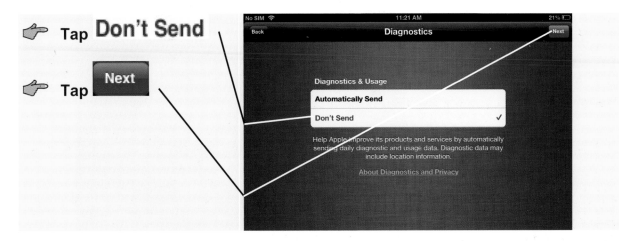

Tap **Don't Send**

Tap **Next**

You have now completed the initial set up. There still is a little more to set up, but that comes later.

Tap
Start Using iPad

Now you will see the home screen with all the colored app icons.

In this screen shot you will see the home screen of the new iPad. The background of the iPad 2 is slightly different.

 Help! My iPad is locked.

If you don't use your iPad for a little while, the home screen will lock itself. This happens after about two minutes of non-activity. You can unlock the iPad like this:

☞ **Press the Home button**

In the bottom of the screen:

👉 **Slide the arrow to the right** ───

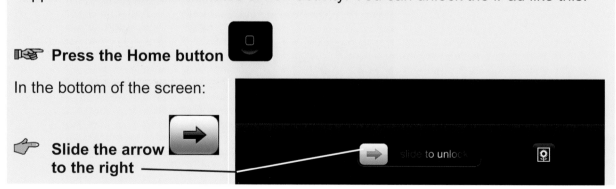

1.3 Connecting the iPad to the Computer

You can connect the iPad to the computer. When it is connected, you can use *iTunes* to sync data, music, videos and more from your computer to the iPad. You can even do this wirelessly with *iTunes Wi-Fi Sync*.

 Please note:

If you have not yet installed *iTunes* onto your computer, it is time to do so now. If you go to *Appendix B Download and Install iTunes* at the end of this book you can read how to do this.

Start the *iTunes* program on your computer, laptop or notebook:

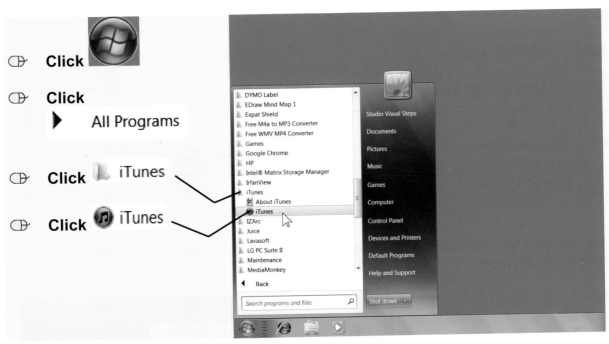

Most likely you will see a window asking you to accept the software license agreement.

You may see a slightly different window on your computer. But this will not affect the following operations.

☞ **Close the window**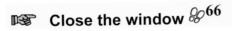

iTunes asks if you want to automatically synchronize your iPad with your *iTunes Library*, as soon as you connect the iPad to the computer. It is better not to do this. Synchronizing means making the content of your iPad equal to the content of your *Library*. Songs, videos, and apps that are not present anymore in your *Library*, will be deleted from your iPad during the synchronizing process. You will have more control over the contents of your iPad if you disable the automatic sync. You can manually start the synchronization when you want to use this option.

☞ **Uncheck the box** ☑ **by**
Automatically sync songs

☞ **Uncheck the box** ☑ **by**
Automatically sync apps t

☞ **Click** ⌐ **Done** ¬

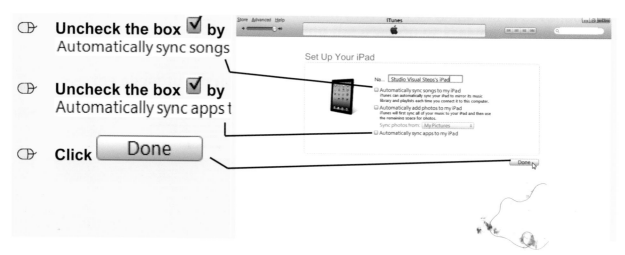

Now you will see the *Summary* tab:

The software on this iPad is up to date: —————

As soon as the iPad is connected, *iTunes* will be opened: —————

☑ Manually manage music and.. means that music and videos will not be synchronized automatically: —————

Here you can see the the amount of memory left on this iPad: —————

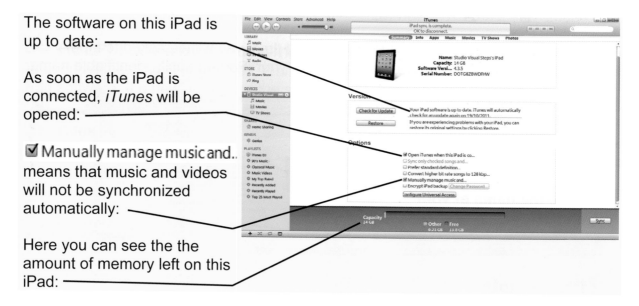

Tip

Sync the iPad wirelessly with iTunes

You have attached your iPad to your computer using the so-called Dock Connector-to-USB cable. You can also synchronize your iPad wirelessly using *iTunes*.

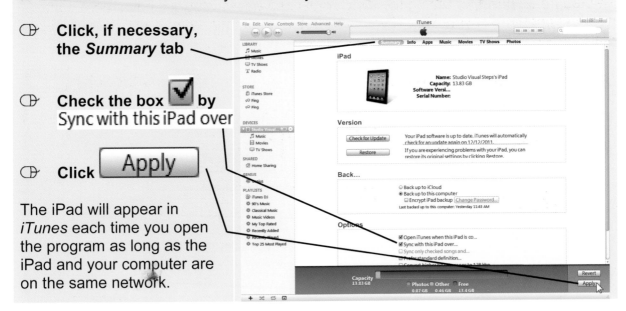

☞ **Click, if necessary, the *Summary* tab**

☞ **Check the box ☑ by** Sync with this iPad over

☞ **Click** Apply

The iPad will appear in *iTunes* each time you open the program as long as the iPad and your computer are on the same network.

To prevent other items, such as e-mail accounts or contacts, from being automatically synchronized, you will need to modify another setting:

☞ **Click** Edit

☞ **Click** Preferences...

You will see a window with various components:

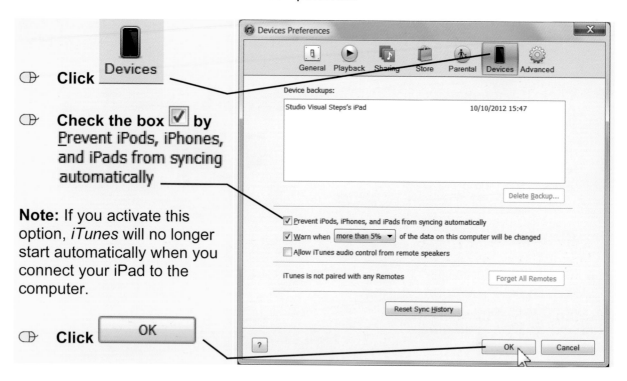

Click **Devices**

Check the box ☑ by Prevent iPods, iPhones, and iPads from syncing automatically

Note: If you activate this option, *iTunes* will no longer start automatically when you connect your iPad to the computer.

Click **OK**

1.5 Safely Disconnecting the iPad

You can disconnect the iPad from your computer any time you want, unless the device is being synchronized with your computer.

If the synchronization is in progress, you will see this message at the top of the *iTunes* window:

> Syncing "Studio Visual Steps's iPad" (Step 2 of 4)
> Preparing to sync

When you see this message, you can disconnect the iPad:

> iPad sync is complete.
> OK to disconnect.

This is how you disconnect your iPad from *iTunes*:

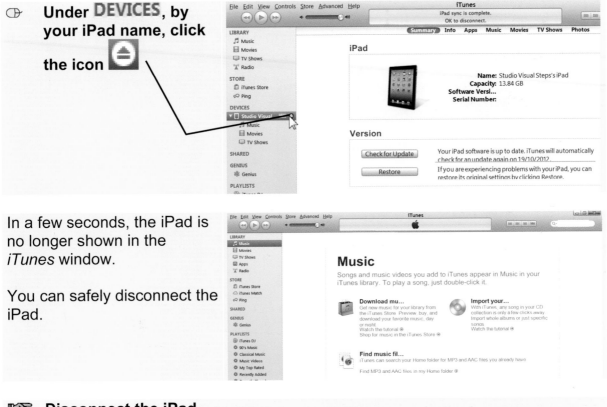

☞ **Under DEVICES, by your iPad name, click the icon** ⏏

In a few seconds, the iPad is no longer shown in the *iTunes* window.

You can safely disconnect the iPad.

☞ **Disconnect the iPad**

You can now close *iTunes*:

☞ **Close *iTunes*** 👣⁶⁶

1.6 The Main Components of Your iPad

In the images below and on the next page you will see the main components of the iPad. When we describe a certain operation in this book, you can look for the relevant component in these images.

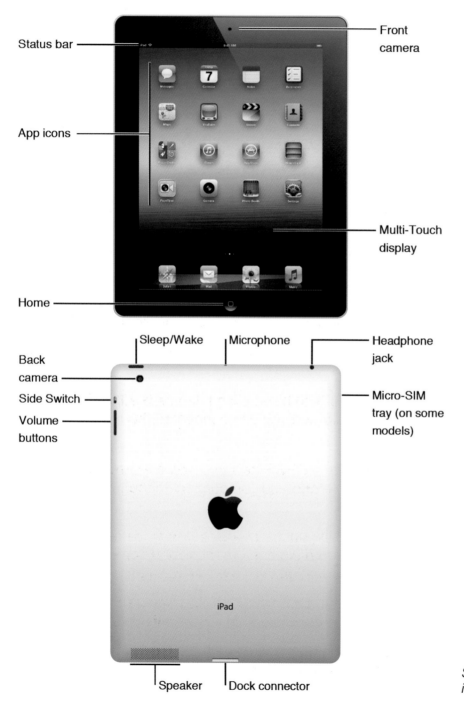

Source:
iPad User Guide

On the status bar, located at the top of your iPad, various icons display information about the status of the iPad and its connections. Below you see an overview of all the status icons you might encounter along with their significance:

🔒 (rotation lock)	This shows that the screen orientation is locked.
🔒 (lock)	The iPad is locked. This icon will be displayed when the lock screen appears.
(battery charging)	Battery is charging.
(battery plug)	Battery is fully charged.
Not Charging	The iPad is connected to the computer, but the USB port does not provide enough power for charging the battery.
▶	Shows that a song, audio book or podcast is playing.
(Wi-Fi)	Shows that the iPad has a Wi-Fi Internet connection. The more bars, the stronger the connection.
No SIM Card Installed	No micro SIM card has been installed (in an iPad suited for Wi-Fi and 3G or 4G).
3G 4G	Shows that your carrier's mobile data network (iPad Wi-Fi + 3G or 4G) is available and you can connect to the Internet over 3G or 4G.
..ıı.. AT&T	Signal strength of the connection and name of the mobile network carrier currently in use.
E	Shows that your carrier's EDGE network (some iPad Wi-Fi + 3G or 4G models) is available and you can connect to the Internet with EDGE.
O	Shows that your carrier's GPRS network (some iPad Wi-Fi + 3G or 4G models) is available and you can connect to the Internet with GPRS.
VPN	This icon appears when you are connected to a *Virtual Private Network* (VPN). VPNs are used in organizations, for secure sending of private information over a public network.
◤	This icon appears when a program uses location services. That means that information about your current location will be used.
✳	Shows network and other activity. Some apps may also use this symbol to indicate an active process.

- Continue on the next page -

Bluetooth icon. If the icon is rendered in grey, it means Bluetooth has been enabled, but no device is connected. If a device is connected, the icon will be displayed in white.

 Airplane mode is on. If your iPad is in this mode, you do not have access to the Internet and you cannot use Bluetooth devices.

1.7 Updating the iPad

Apple is regularly issuing new updates for the iPad software. In these updates, existing problems are fixed or new functions are added. You can just check if there are any updates available for your iPad. If necessary, wake your iPad up from sleep:

 Press the Home button

You will see the locked screen of the iPad. This is how you unlock the iPad and proceed to the home screen:

☞ **Drag the slider to the right**

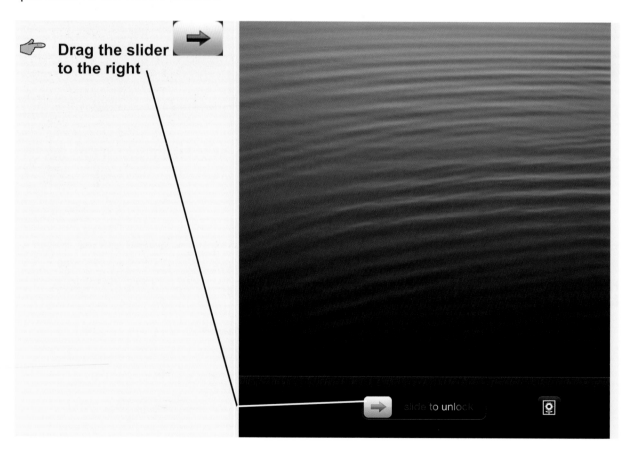

Now you will see the home screen of your iPad. This is how to open the *Settings* app:

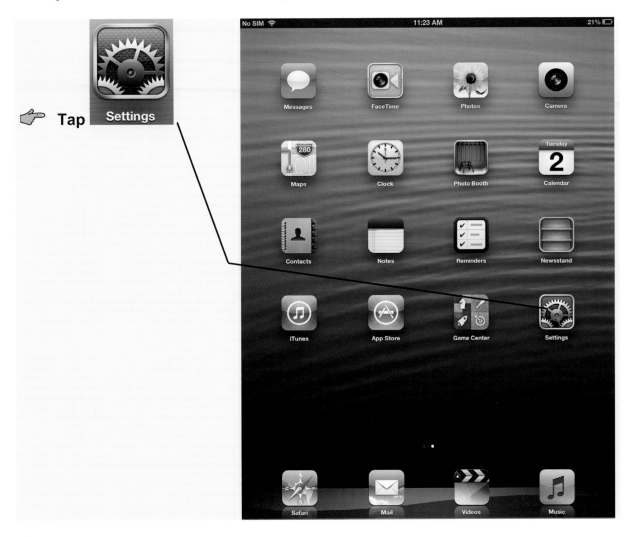

☞ **Tap** Settings

Please note:

In this book we always use the iPad in portrait mode, where the longer side is vertically positioned. We recommend using your iPad in portrait mode while you work through the chapters in this book, otherwise you may see a screen that is different from the examples shown.

Here you see the *Settings* app:

The *General* section is already opened:

☞ Tap **Software Update**

Now the iPad will check if there is any new software available.

In this example, the iPad already has the current software version installed:

To return to the *General* section:

☞ Tap **General**

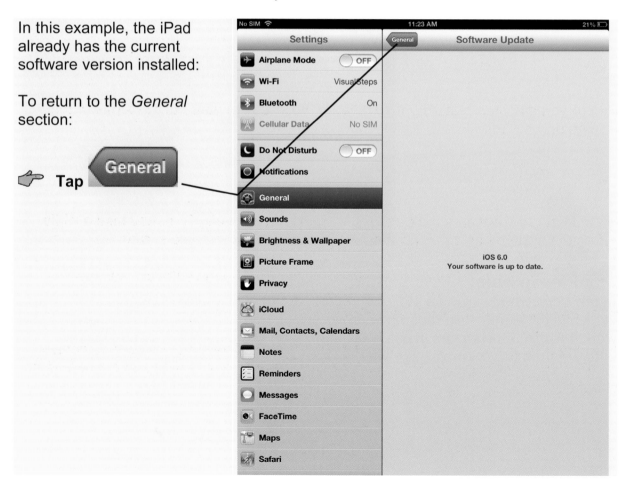

If a newer version is found, you will see this screen:

Tap

Install

Before you can start installing the software, you need to agree to the terms of the license agreement:

Tap Agree

Your screen will become dark and the installation will begin. This may take a while. When the update has been installed, you will return to the home screen.

If slightly different windows are displayed while installing the software update:

☞ Follow the onscreen instructions

It is also possible to install a new update with *iTunes*. Then you will need to connect the iPad to your computer. You can read more about this in the *Tips* at the end of this chapter.

1.8 Basic iPad Operations

In this section, you will learn how easy it is to use your iPad. You will practice some basic operations and touch movements. If necessary, wake your iPad up from sleep:

☞ **Press the Home button**

You will see the locked screen of the iPad. This is how you unlock the iPad and proceed to the home screen:

☞ **Drag the slider**
to the right

Now you will see the home screen of your iPad. This is how to open the *Settings* app:

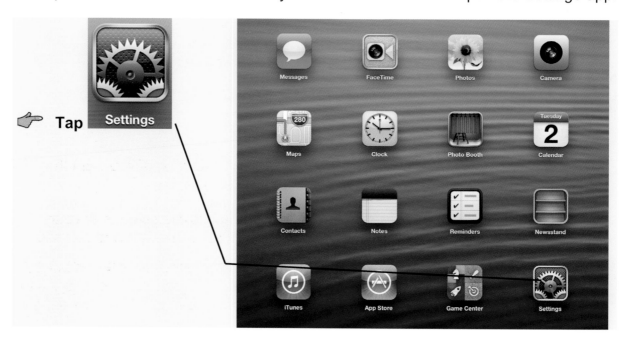

☞ **Tap** **Settings**

The iPad Side Switch can be used in two different ways:
- *Lock Rotation*: lock the screen in portrait or in landscape mode.
- *Mute*: mute the sound of messages and other sound effects.

By default, the Mute function is enabled. This is how you can use the Side Switch to lock the rotation:

☞ **If necessary, slide the side switch upwards**

Now you can check to see if this works:

☞ **Hold the iPad upright, in a vertical position**

☞ **Turn the iPad to the right or left towards a horizontal position**

☞ **Hold the iPad upright again**

You will see that the position of the screen orients itself to the position of the iPad.

☞ **Slide the side switch downwards**

You will see this icon:

Now the iPad is locked in vertical position.

☞ **Turn the iPad across to a horizontal position**

Now you will see that the image on the iPad screen is not rotating. If you want the iPad screen to rotate, you can slide the side switch upwards again.

You can adapt the background (Wallpaper) of the lock and home screens of your iPad to your own taste, by selecting a different background. Here is how to do that:

☞ **Tap**
  Brightness & Wallpap

With this slider you can adjust the brightness of the screen:

By default, the brightness of the screen is automatically adapted to the light of the environment. This is indicated by the **ON** button:

Here is how to change the wallpaper:

☞ **Tap**

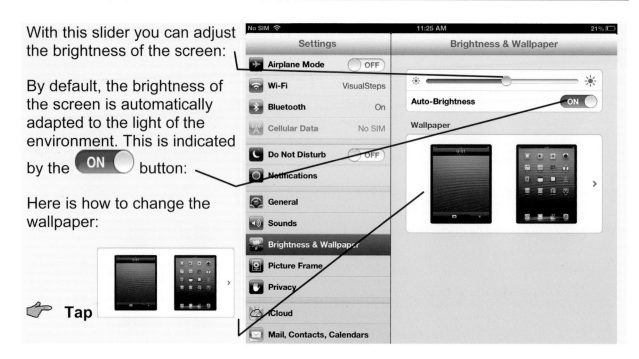

Select a wallpaper from one of the standard *Apple* wallpapers:

☞ **Tap**

　Wallpaper

If you do not see this window:

☞ **Continue with the next step**

☞ **Tap a wallpaper, for instance**

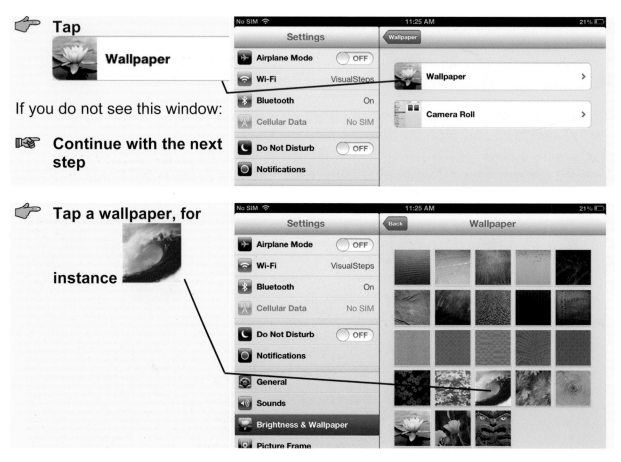

You will see a preview of this wallpaper. Now you can decide if you want to use this wallpaper for the lock screen, the home screen, or both:

Now you will be back at the *Brightness and Wallpaper* screen. Check to see if the wallpaper of the lock screen has indeed been changed.
Here is how to close the *Settings* app:

Put the iPad in sleep mode:

☞ **Tap the Sleep/Wake button**

☞ **Wake the iPad up from sleep mode** 👣²

Now you will see that the wallpaper of the lock screen has been changed.

1.9 Using the Keyboard

Your iPad contains a useful onscreen keyboard, which will appear whenever you need to type something. For example, if you want to take notes in the *Notes* app. Here is how to open the *Notes* app:

You will see a new, blank notes page:

Tap the first line

The onscreen keyboard will appear:

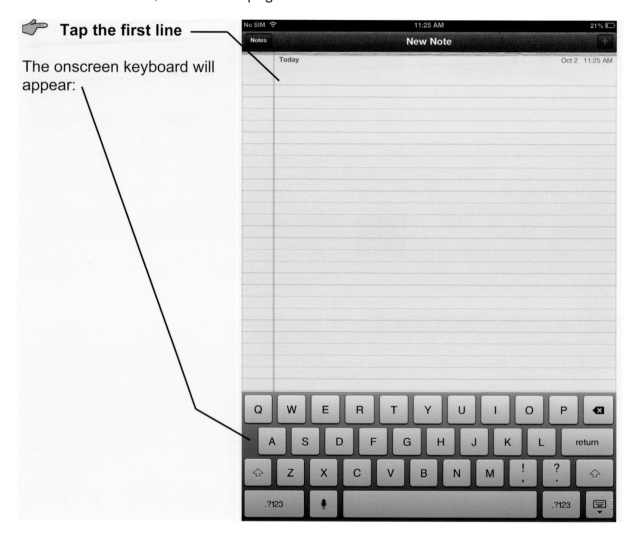

The onscreen keyboard works almost the same way as a regular keyboard. You simply tap the keys instead of pressing them. Just give it a try:

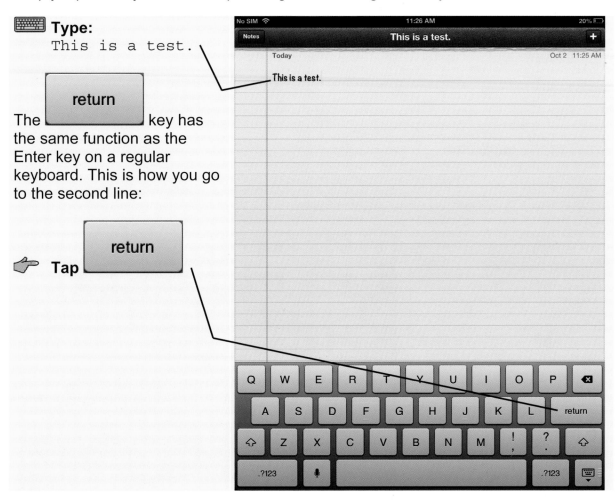

Type:
This is a test.

The key has the same function as the Enter key on a regular keyboard. This is how you go to the second line:

👉 **Tap** return

💡 **Tip**

Comma, period, exclamation mark, question mark

The comma and the exclamation mark share a key on the keyboard, just as the period and the question mark. This is how to type the symbol on the lower part of the key, for example, the period:

👉 **Tap**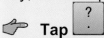

And this is how to type the symbol on the upper part of the key, for example, the question mark:

👉 **Tap** ⇧

👉 **Tap**

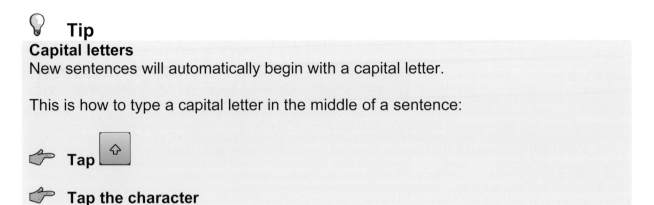

In the standard view of the keyboard, you will not see any numerals. If you want to use numerals, you need to change the keyboard view:

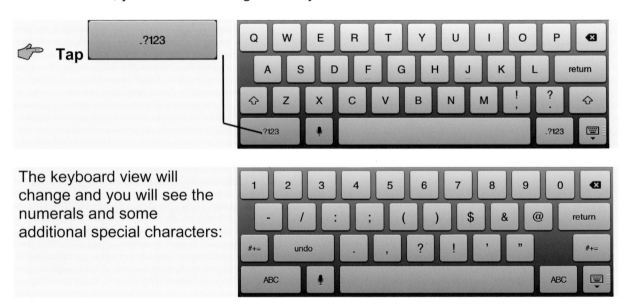

👉 **Tap** .?123

The keyboard view will change and you will see the numerals and some additional special characters:

Type the beginning of an easy sum:

⌨ **Type:** 12-10

To type the '=' sign you need to use the third view of the onscreen keyboard:

👉 **Tap** #+=

Now you will see yet another view of the keyboard:

Finish the sum:

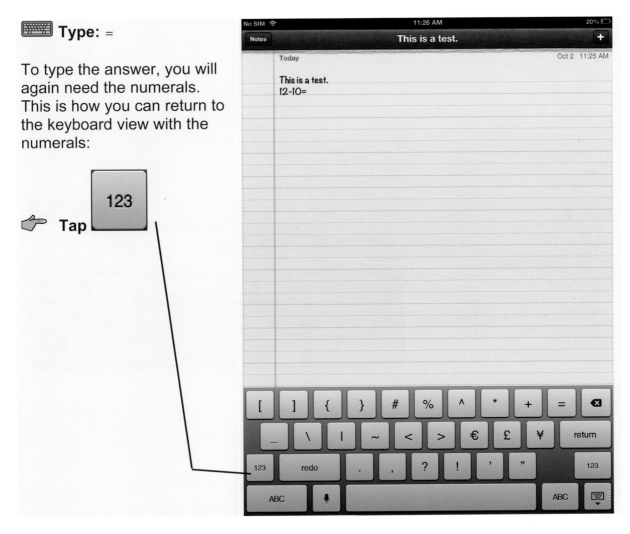

Type: =

To type the answer, you will again need the numerals. This is how you can return to the keyboard view with the numerals:

Tap **123**

Now you will see the keyboard with the numerals and special characters once again:

Type: 3

If you have made a typing error, you can correct this with the Backspace key:

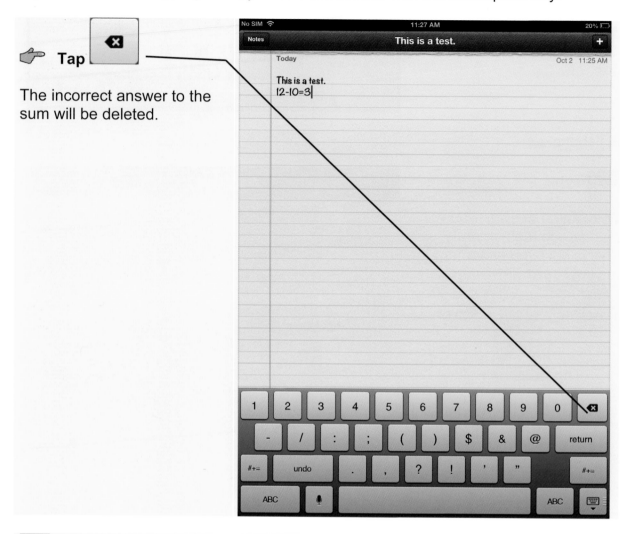

☞ **Tap**

The incorrect answer to the sum will be deleted.

 Type: 2

Now the answer is correct.

💡 **Tip**

Return to the standard keyboard view
If you are in the view with the numerals and special characters, you can go back to the standard onscreen keyboard with the letters:

☞ **Tap**

Now you are going to delete the note. First, you are going to hide the keyboard:

 Tap

The onscreen keyboard has disappeared.

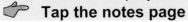

💡 Tip

Display the keyboard on the screen again
This is how to display the keyboard again:
👉 **Tap the notes page**

This is how you delete the note:

👉 Tap 🗑

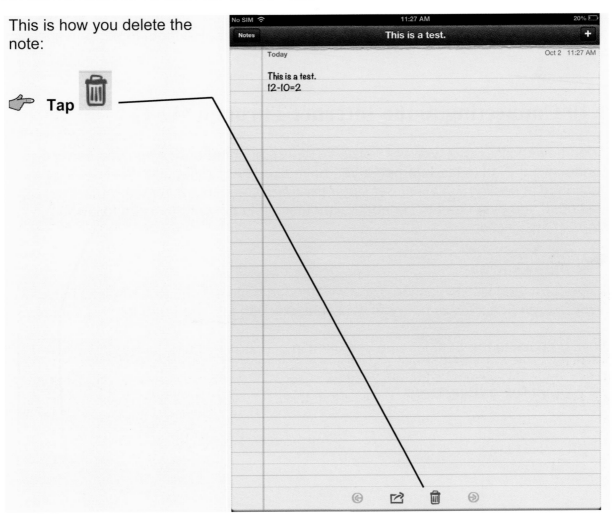

You will need to confirm the deletion:

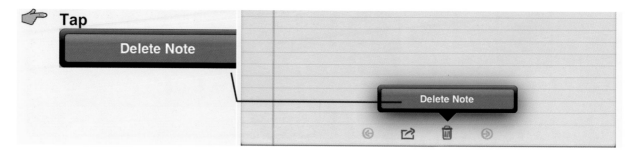

Now you can close the *Notes* app:

 Press the Home button

By now, you have practiced some of the basic operations and touch actions. There are more touch actions to learn, such as scrolling and zooming in and out. We will discuss these actions in the chapters where you need to use them to perform specific tasks.

1.10 Connecting to the Internet Through Wi-Fi

If you have access to a wireless network (Wi-Fi), at home or at work, you can connect your iPad to the Internet. If you have already modified the Wi-Fi settings as described in *section 1.2 Initial Set Up of the iPad*, you can just read through this section. If you ever need to connect to another Wi-Fi network you can follow the steps in this section.

Please note:

To perform the following actions, you will need to have access to a wireless network (Wi-Fi). If Wi-Fi access is not (yet) available, you can just read through this section.

Now, go back to the *Settings* app you used in previous steps:

Open the *Settings* app ⚹⚹[6]

You will try to connect to a Wi-Fi network:

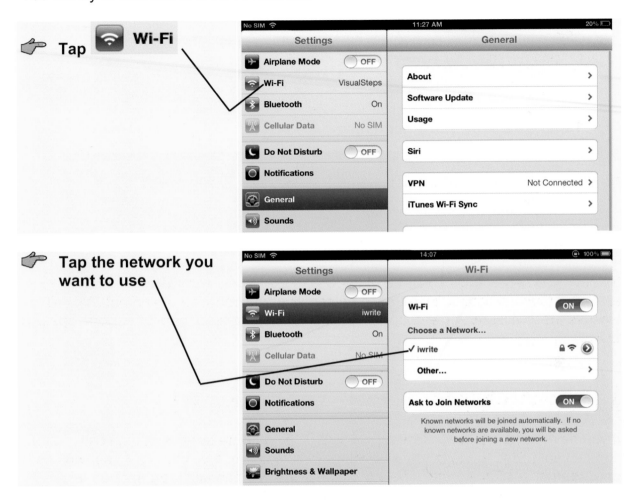

You will be connected to the wireless network:

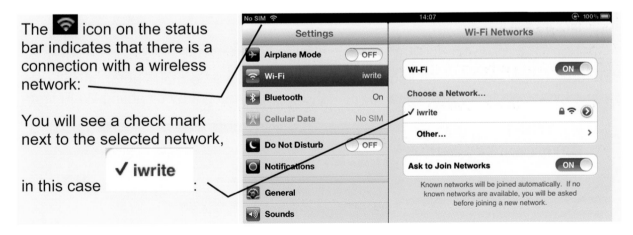

💡 Tip

Secure network

If you see a padlock icon next to the network name, for instance

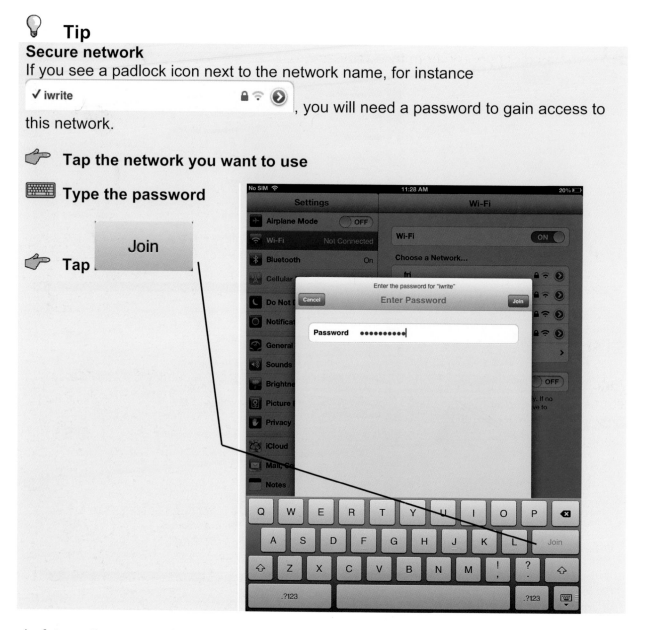

, you will need a password to gain access to this network.

👉 **Tap the network you want to use**

⌨ **Type the password**

👉 **Tap** Join

In future, the connection with known wireless networks will be made automatically as soon as you enable Wi-Fi. You can check this out for yourself by disabling Wi-Fi first:

👉 **By Wi-Fi, tap the ON button**

Now, Wi-Fi is disabled and you will see that the button looks like this ⬭ OFF . The 📶 icon has disappeared from the status bar.

👉 By **Wi-Fi** , tap the ⬭ OFF button

Wi-Fi will be enabled once again.

Automatically, the iPad will connect to the wireless network you were previously using:

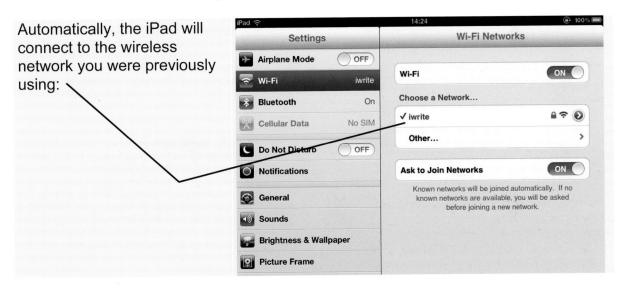

👉 **If you want, you can disable Wi-Fi again** 🐾[7]

👉 **Press the Home button**

1.11 Connecting to the Internet Through the Mobile Data Network

If your iPad is also suitable for the mobile data network, you can connect it to a 3G or 4G network. The 4G network is only available in the United States. Connecting to the mobile data network can be useful when you are in a location where there is no Wi-Fi. You will need to have a micro SIM card with a data subscription or contract, or a prepaid mobile Internet card. If you do not (yet) have these items, you can just read through this section.

 Tip

Mobile Internet
Since the iPad does not have a simlock, you are free to select a mobile Internet provider. Many providers, such as AT&T, Verizon Wireless and British Telecom offer data subscriptions for the iPad, including a micro SIM card. For prepaid mobile Internet plans you can use Virgin Mobile USA, AT&T, Verizon and Vodafone, among others.

The prices and conditions are subject to regular changes. Check out the websites of various providers for more information.

An iPad that is suitable for Wi-Fi and 3G or 4G will be fitted with a micro SIM card tray.

Remove the micro SIM card tray, by using the SIM eject tool (included in the packaging):

If you do not have this tool, you can also use the end of a small paperclip.

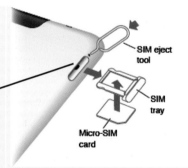

Source: User Guide iPad

☞ **Place the micro SIM card in the micro SIM card tray**

☞ **Insert the micro SIM card tray into the iPad**

The connection with the mobile data network will start up automatically.

As soon as the connection has been made, you will see the signal strength and the name of the mobile network provider in use:

If the iPad status bar displays the 3G (**3G**) or 4G (**4G**), EDGE (**E**), or GPRS (**O**) symbols, the device is connected to the Internet through the mobile data network.

If necessary, you can temporarily disable the Internet connection through the mobile data network. This way, you can prevent your children or grandchildren from playing online games on your iPad and using up all of your prepaid credit. Here is how to do that:

☞ **Open the *Settings* app** ✂⁶

👉 **Tap** 📡 **Cellular Data**

👉 **By Cellular Data, tap** **ON** ⬤

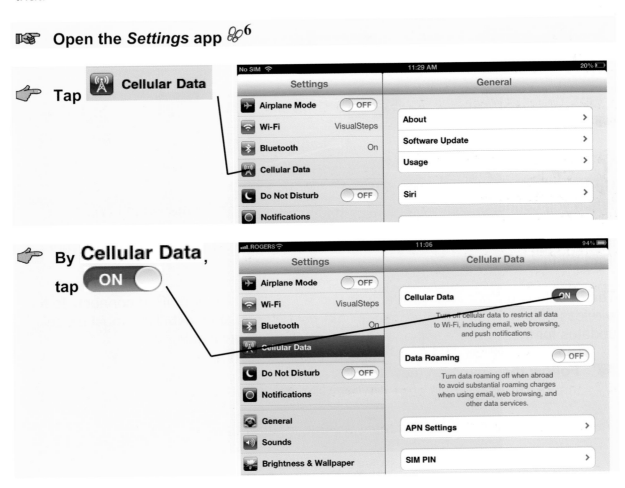

In future, you can decide whether you want to put the iPad in sleep mode, or turn it off. In this chapter you have learned how to turn the iPad on and off, connect and disconnect it to the computer and how to gain access to the Internet. You have also taken a closer look at some of the main components of the iPad and performed basic operations for using the device.

The exercises on the following page will let you practice these operations. In the *Background Information* and the *Tips* you will find additional information for this chapter.

1.13 Exercises

To be able to quickly apply the things you have learned, you can work through these exercises. Have you forgotten how to do something? Use the numbers next to the footsteps 🐾¹ to look up the item in the appendix *How Do I Do That Again?*

Exercise 1: Turn On, Sleep Mode and Turn Off

In this exercise you are going to repeat turning the iPad on and off, and putting it into sleep mode.

☞ If necessary, wake up the iPad from sleep mode, or turn it on. 🐾²

☞ Put the iPad into sleep mode. 🐾¹

☞ Wake up the iPad up from sleep mode. 🐾²

☞ Turn off the iPad. 🐾¹

Exercise 2: The Onscreen Keyboard

In this exercise you are going to type a short text with the onscreen keyboard.

☞ Turn on the iPad. 🐾²

☞ Open the *Notes* app. 🐾³

☞ Type the following text: 🐾⁴
The distance between New York and Boston is 189 miles. The distance between New York and Buffalo is 395 miles. How long would that take by car?

☞ Delete the note. 🐾⁵

☞ If you want, put the iPad into sleep mode, or turn it off. 🐾¹

1.14 Background Information

Dictionary

Accelerometer	A sensor that registers whether the position of the iPad is in the vertical (portrait) or horizontal (landscape) orientation.
Airplane mode	If your iPad is in this mode, you will not have access to the Internet and will not be able to use Bluetooth devices.
App	Short for *application*, a program for the iPad.
App icons	Colored icons on the iPad, used to open various apps.
App Store	Online store where you can download apps, for free or at a price.
Auto-Lock	A function that makes sure the iPad is turned off and locked after two minutes (by default), if it is not in use.
Bluetooth	Bluetooth is an open wireless technology standard for exchanging data over short distances. With Bluetooth you can connect a wireless keyboard or headset to the iPad, for example.
Data roaming	Using the wireless network of another provider, when your own carrier's network is not available. Using this option abroad may lead to high costs.
EDGE	Short for *Enhanced Data Rates for GSM Evolution*. It allows improved data transmission rates as a backward-compatible extension of GSM. In the UK, EDGE coverage is reasonably widespread and in the USA it is pretty common.
GPRS	Short for *General Packet Radio Service*, a technology that is an extension of the existing gsm network. This technology makes it possible to transfer wireless data more efficiently, faster and cheaper.
Gyroscope	A sensor that measures in which direction the iPad is moving. Some games use this function.

- Continue on the next page -

Home button	, the button that lets you return to the home screen. You can also use this button to wake the iPad up from sleep.
Home screen	The screen with the app icons. This is what you see when you turn the iPad on or unlock it.
iPad	The iPad is a portable multimedia device (a tablet computer) made by Apple. The iPad is a computer with a multi-touch screen.
iTunes	A program that lets you manage the content of your iPad. But you can also use *iTunes* to listen to music files, watch movies, and import CDs. In *iTunes* you will also find the *iTunes Store* and the *App Store*.
iTunes Store	Online store where you can download and purchase music, movies, tv shows, podcasts, audio books and more.
Library	The *iTunes* section where you can store and manage your music, movies, podcasts and apps.
Location Services	Location Services lets apps such as *Maps* gather and use data showing your location. For example, if you are connected to the Internet and have turned on Location Services, data about the location will be added to the photos and videos you take with your iPad.
Lock screen	The screen you see when you turn the iPad on. Before you can use the iPad, you need to unlock it by swiping the slider.
Micro SIM card	The small SIM card that is used in the iPad Wi-Fi + 3G or 4G, for wireless data transfer. This SIM card is also called a 3FF SIM card (Third Form Factor).
Notes	An app with which you can take notes.
Podcast	An episodic program, delivered through the Internet. Podcast episodes can be audio or video files and can be downloaded with the *iTunes Store*.
Rotation lock	This function takes care of locking the screen display when you rotate the iPad.

- Continue on the next page -

Simlock

A simlock is a capability built into a cell phone or another wireless device that is used to restrict the use of the SIM card for that device. This lock prevents the user from using SIM cards from different providers in the device. The reason many network providers SIM lock their phones is that they offer phones at a discount to customers in exchange for a contract to pay for the use of the network for a specified time period, usually between one and three years. The iPad Wi-Fi + 3G or 4G is simlock free.

Sleep mode

You can lock the iPad by putting it into sleep mode if you do not use it for a while. When the iPad is locked, it will not react when you touch the screen. But you can still keep on playing music. And you can still use the volume buttons. You can activate or deactivate sleep mode with the Sleep/Wake button.

Synchronize

Literally, this means: equalizing. If you sync your iPad with your *iTunes Library*, the content of your iPad will be made equal to the content of your *Library* on your computer. If you delete files or apps from your *Library*, these will also be deleted from the iPad, when you synchronize it again.

Tablet computer

A tablet computer is a computer without casing and a separate keyboard. It is operated by a multi-touch screen.

VPN

Short for *Virtual Private Network*. With VPN you can gain access to private secure networks through the Internet, such as your company network.

Wi-Fi

Wireless network for the Internet.

3G

3G is the third generation of standards and technology for cell phones. Because of its higher speed, 3G offers extensive possibilities. For example, with 3G you can use services such as making phone calls via the Internet, among others.

4G

4G is the fourth generation of standards and technology for cell phones. It is almost ten times the speed of 3G and will offer many new possibilities. At the moment of writing, 4G is only available in the United States.

Source: User Guide iPad, Wikipedia

1.15 Tips

 Tip

Auto-Lock

By default, the iPad will lock and go into sleep mode after two minutes, if you do not use it, or it is left unattended. This setting will save energy, but maybe you would prefer to keep the iPad on for a little longer:

☞ **Open the *Settings* app** 👣⁶

👉 **Tap** Auto-Lock

On this page you can set a different duration:

👉 **Tap the desired time setting**

💡 **Tip**

Type faster
This is how you can quickly type a period and a blank space at the end of a sentence:

☞ **Double-tap the space bar twice, quickly**

💡 **Tip**

Enable Caps Lock
If you only want to use capitals:

☞ **Double-tap**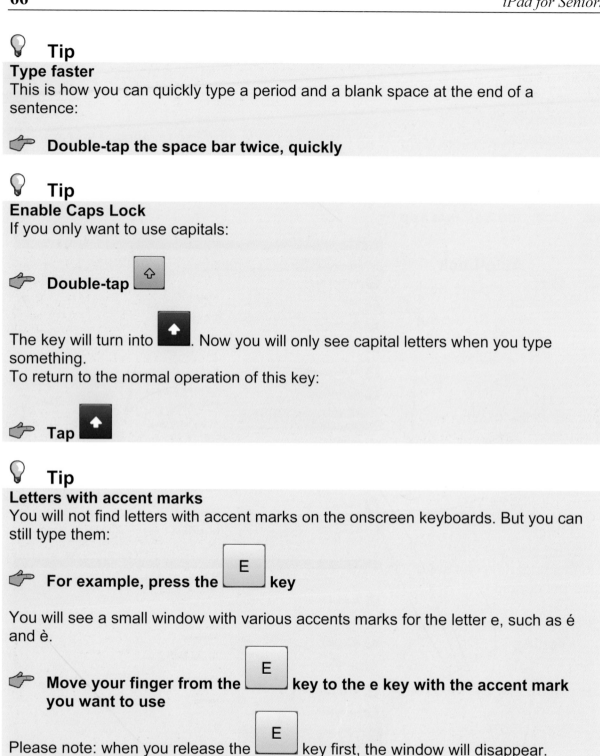

The key will turn into 🔼. Now you will only see capital letters when you type something.
To return to the normal operation of this key:

☞ **Tap** 🔼

💡 **Tip**

Letters with accent marks
You will not find letters with accent marks on the onscreen keyboards. But you can still type them:

☞ **For example, press the** E **key**

You will see a small window with various accents marks for the letter e, such as é and è.

☞ **Move your finger from the** E **key to the e key with the accent mark you want to use**

Please note: when you release the E key first, the window will disappear.

☞ **Release the key**

The e with the accent mark will appear in the text.

Tip

Larger keys

If you disable the rotation
lock and position the iPad
horizontally, the keys on the
onscreen keyboard will
become larger:

 Tip

Updating the iPad with iTunes

If you don't have access to a Wi-Fi network and you need to perform a software
update, you can do that through *iTunes*.

☞ **Open *iTunes*** 𝄞100

⊕ **Click**

Check for Update

If a new update is available:

⊕ **Click** Update

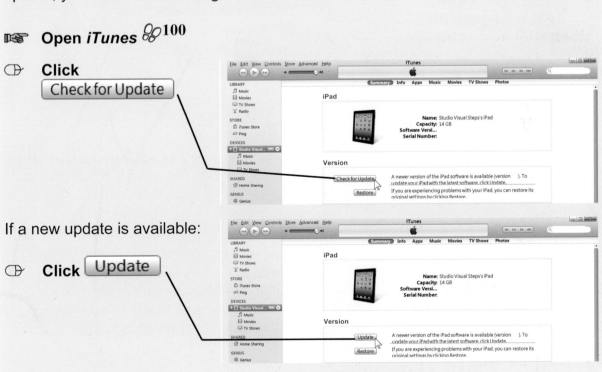

- Continue on the next page -

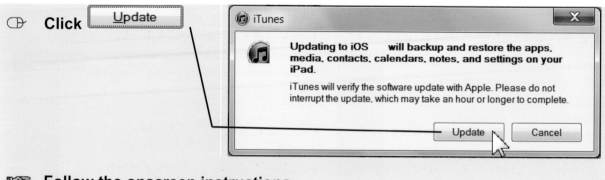

Click [Update]

☞ **Follow the onscreen instructions**

💡 **Tip**
Backup copy
If you chose not to synchronize your iPad with *iTunes* each time you connect it to your computer, you will not be creating an automatic backup. A backup will contain the iPad's system settings, app data, Camera Roll album, and more. Things that you put on your iPad by way of *iTunes*, such as music, movies, podcasts and more remain in the *iTunes* data folders. It is important that you backup your computer now and then as well. You can make a backup of the iPad by doing the following:

☞ **Connect the iPad to the computer**

⊕ **Under DEVICES,**
right-click your iPad
name

⊕ **Select** Back Up

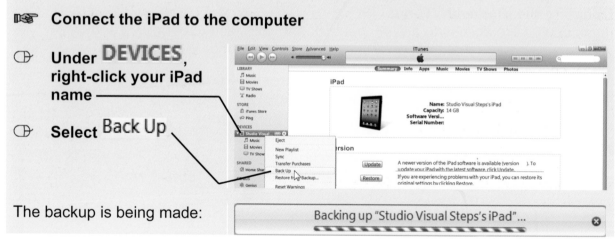

The backup is being made:

💡 **Tip**
iCloud
One of Apple's latest developments is the *iCloud* service. At the moment of writing, this function was still being developed. The *iCloud* is a so-called cloud computing service, like a hard drive in the sky. With this function you can store content such as photos, music, apps, contacts and calendars. This way your content is available for download to different devices such as the iPad, iPhone, iPod touch and Mac.

2. Sending E-mails with Your iPad

Your iPad contains a standard e-mail app called *Mail.*

With *Mail* you can send, receive and compose e-mail messages, just like on your regular computer. In this chapter you can read how to adjust the settings for your e-mail account. We will explain how to do this for Internet service providers (ISP), such as Charter, Comcast, Cox, AT & T or Verizon and also for web-based email services such as *Windows Live Hotmail.* If you use multiple e-mail accounts, you can configure each one to work with the *Mail* program.

Composing an e-mail on your iPad is quite easy. You will have lots of opportunity to practice this by working though this chapter. You will learn how to select, copy, cut, and paste items using the iPad screen. You will also become familiar with the autocorrect function that is built into the iPad.

Later on this chapter, we will explain how to send, receive and delete e-mail messages.

In this chapter you will learn how to:

- set up an e-mail account;
- set up a *Hotmail* account;
- send an e-mail;
- receive an e-mail;
- move an e-mail to the *Recycle Bin*;
- permanently delete an e-mail.

Now you will see a screen where you need to enter some basic information concerning your e-mail account. To do this, you can use the onscreen keyboard from the iPad:

Type your name

By Address, enter your e-mail address

Type your password

By Description, type an identifiable name for your e-mail account

When you have finished entering the information:

Tap Next

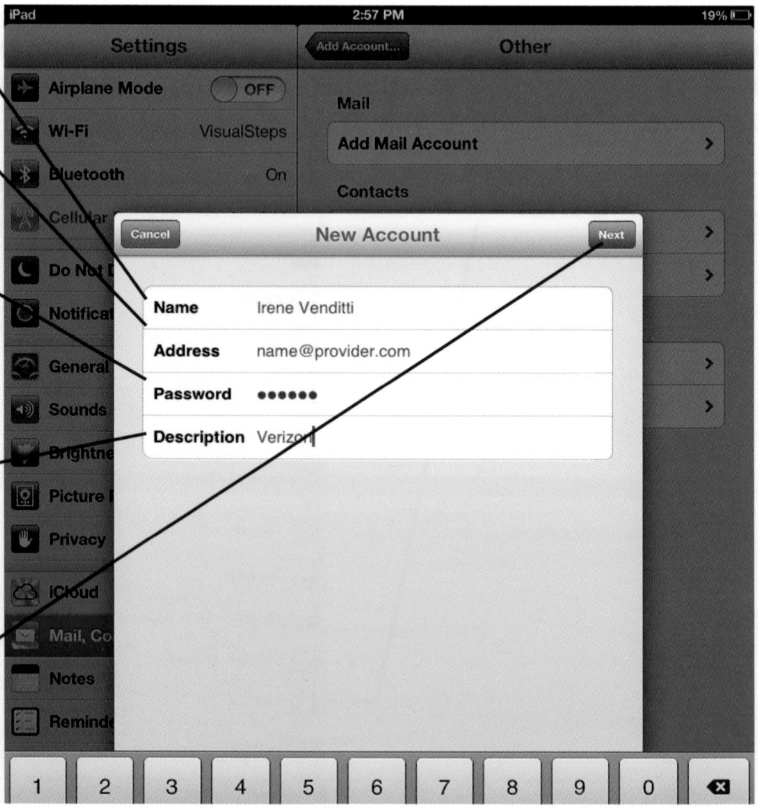

Tip

Onscreen keyboard

Have you forgotten how to use the iPad onscreen keyboard? Go back to *section 1.9 Using the Keyboard*.

Now you can select whether you want to set your e-mail account as an *IMAP* or a *POP* account:

- IMAP stands for *Internet Message Access Protocol*. This means that you will manage your messages on the mail server. Messages that have been read will be stored on the mail server, until you delete them. IMAP is useful if you manage your e-mails from multiple computers. Your mailbox will look the same on each computer. When you create folders for organizing your e-mail messages, you will see the same folders on the other computers as well as your iPad. If you want to use IMAP, you will need to set your e-mail account as an IMAP account on all the other computers too.
- POP stands for *Post Office Protocol*, the traditional way of managing e-mail. When you retrieve your messages, they will immediately be deleted from the

server. Although, on your iPad the default setting for POP accounts is for a copy to be stored on the server, after you have retrieved a message. This means you will still be able to retrieve the message on your other computer(s). In the *Tips* at the back of this chapter you can read how to modify these settings.

☞ Tap **POP** or **IMAP**

By **Incoming Mail Server**.

⌨ By **Host Name** type the name of the incoming mail server

⌨ By **User Name** type the user name

By **Outgoing Mail Server**.

⌨ By **Host Name** type the name of the outgoing mail server

If by **Outgoing Mail Server** you see the text *Optional* in the fields for the user name and password, you do not need to enter this information.

☞ Tap **Save**

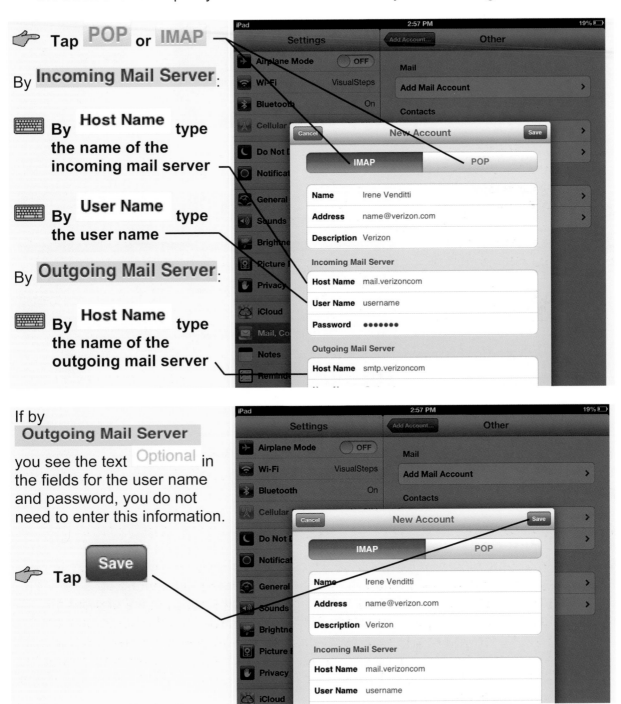

Your account information will be verified. This may take several minutes. You may see a message that the device cannot connect through SSL (*Secure Sockets Layer*). This is a security protocol for Internet traffic.

👉 **Tap**

If you see the same message again:

👉 **Tap**

Now your e-mail account has been added:

☞ **Go back to the home screen** 👣⁸

 HELP! It does not work.

Because of the growing popularity of the iPad and the iPhone, many providers such as AT&T and AOL have put instructions on their websites about setting up an e-mail account for the iPad. Just look for something like 'e-mail settings iPad' on your provider's website and follow the instructions listed.

2.2 Setting Up a Hotmail Account

If you have a *Windows Live Hotmail* account, you can set this up on your iPad too.
Please note: you can set up a Gmail account on a similar way.

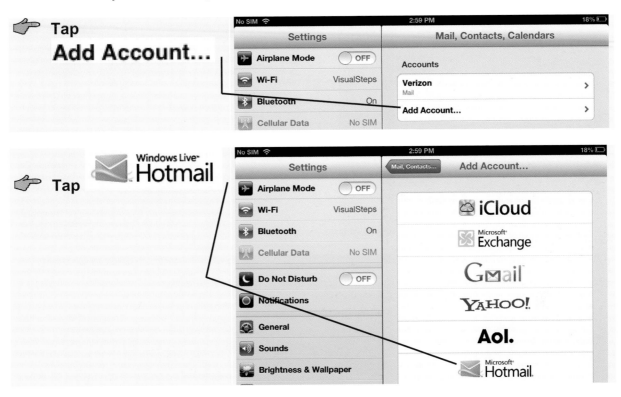

☞ **Tap** **Add Account...**

☞ **Tap** Windows Live Hotmail

In this example we have used an e-mail address that ends with hotmail.com.

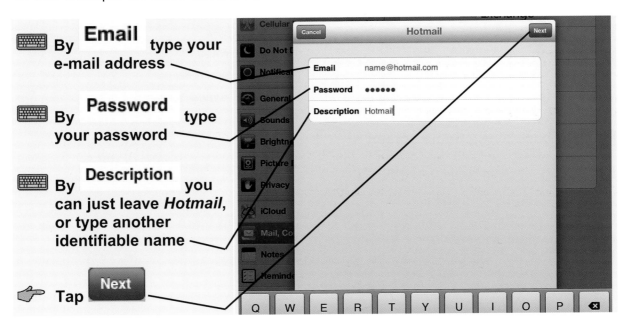

⌨ By **Email** type your e-mail address

⌨ By **Password** type your password

⌨ By **Description** you can just leave *Hotmail*, or type another identifiable name

☞ **Tap** **Next**

The iPad will recognize the *Hotmail* server automatically.

On this page you can select an option to synchronize your contacts and calendars too, besides your e-mail. By default, these options are enabled:

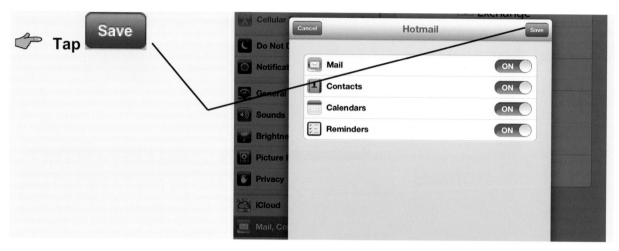

☞ Tap Save

You will see that the *Hotmail* account has been added:

 Go back to the home screen 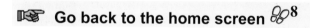⁸

💡 **Tip**

Multiple e-mail accounts
Do you have multiple e-mail accounts? Then you can set them all up on your iPad. Follow the steps in *section 2.1 Setting Up an E-mail Account* or *2.2 Setting Up a Hotmail Account* and individually set up each account.

2.3 Sending an E-mail

Just for practice, you are going to write an e-mail message to yourself. First, you need to open the *Mail* app:

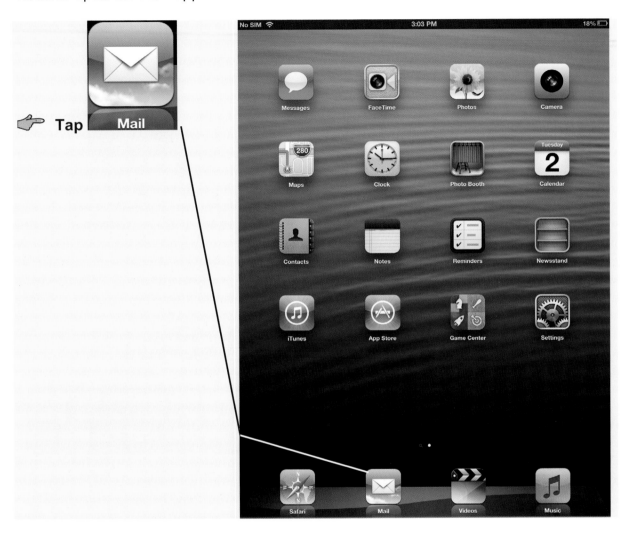

Tap **Mail**

The app will immediately check for new messages. In this example there are not any new messages, but your own mail app may contain some new messages. You are going to open a new, blank e-mail:

Tap

A new message will be opened.

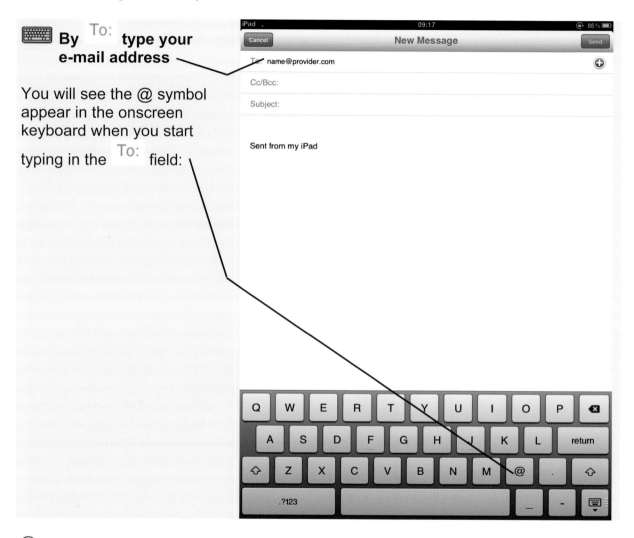

By To: **type your e-mail address**

You will see the @ symbol appear in the onscreen keyboard when you start typing in the To: field:

💡 **Tip**

Contacts

You can use the ⊕ button to open the list of contacts. You can select the recipient from this list by tapping his or her name.

In *Chapter 4 The Standard Apps on Your iPad* you will learn how to enter contacts in the list with the *Contacts* app.

☞ **Tap** Subject:

⌨ **Type:** Test

☞ **Tap the white area where you want to type your message**

⌨ **Type:** This is a test.

Continue on a new line:

☞ **Tap** return

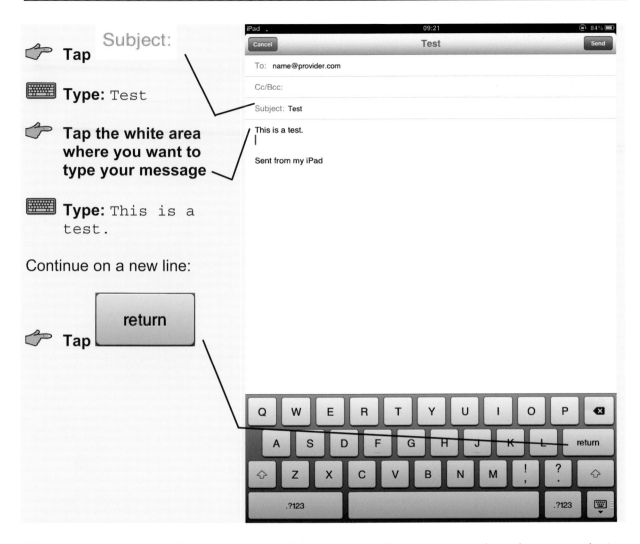

The iPad contains a dictionary that will help you while you are typing. Just see what happens when you intentionally make a spelling mistake:

⌨ **Type:** Type a speling mistake

You will see that the correct spelling is suggested while you are typing:

You can accept the suggested correction without stopping, just continue typing:

 Type a blank space

You will see that the mistake is corrected:

 Tip

Accept correction
A suggested correction will also be accepted if you type a period, comma or another punctuation symbol.

 Tip

Refuse correction
You can also refuse to accept a suggested correction. This is how you do it:

☞ **Tap the correction** spelling ×

You need to do this before you type a blank space, period, comma or other punctuation symbol, otherwise the correction will be accepted.

 Tip

Turn off Autocorrect
In the *Tips* at the back of this chapter you can read how to disable the auto correction function while typing.

If you are not satisfied with your text, you can erase the text quickly with the Backspace key:

☞ **Press your finger on**

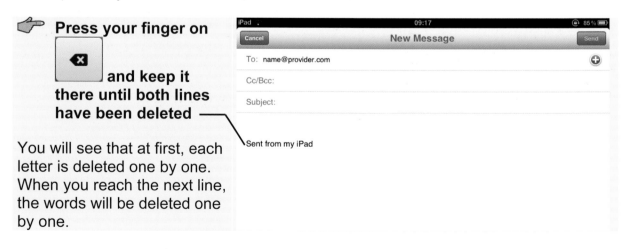

and keep it there until both lines have been deleted

You will see that at first, each letter is deleted one by one. When you reach the next line, the words will be deleted one by one.

In *Mail* you can also copy, cut and paste. You can only do this with an entire word, multiple words or the entire text. Here is how you select a word:

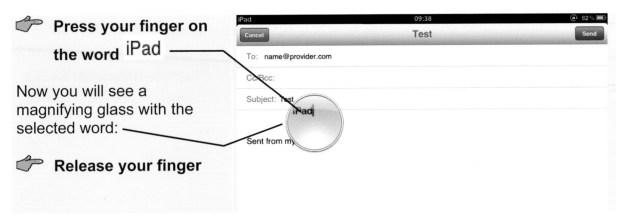

☞ **Press your finger on**

   the word iPad

Now you will see a magnifying glass with the selected word:

☞ **Release your finger**

Now you can choose whether you want to select a single word or the entire text. You are going to select the word:

☞ **Tap** Select

💡 **Tip**

Magnifying glass

With the magnifying glass, you can easily position the cursor on the exact spot inside a word, or between two words. This is helpful when you want to edit or correct text. Move your finger along, until you can see the correct position of the cursor in the magnifying glass, then release your finger. You will not need to use the

Select   or   Select All   buttons. You can just go on typing.

The word has been selected. To select multiple words, you can move the pins ⌐ and

⌐. Now you can cut or copy it, or replace it by a similar word. You are going to copy the word:

☞ Tap **Copy**

The word has been copied to the clipboard. This is how you paste it in the text:

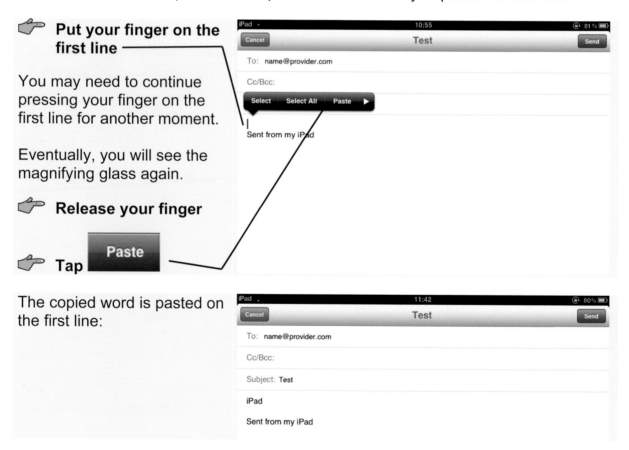

☞ **Put your finger on the first line**

You may need to continue pressing your finger on the first line for another moment.

Eventually, you will see the magnifying glass again.

☞ **Release your finger**

☞ Tap **Paste**

The copied word is pasted on the first line:

It is also possible to format the text in an e-mail message. For example, you can render words in bold or in italics. In the *Tips* at the back of this chapter you can read how to do this.

Now you can send your test e-mail message:

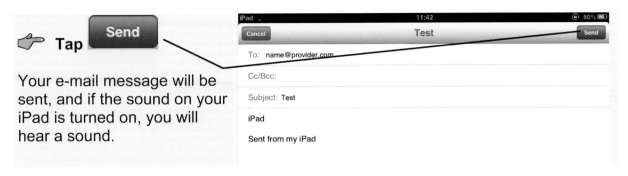

Your e-mail message will be sent, and if the sound on your iPad is turned on, you will hear a sound.

2.4 Receiving an E-mail

Shortly afterwards, your message will be received. You may hear another sound signal. This is how you open the *Inbox* folder, where your incoming messages are stored:

The number on the  button indicates how many new messages you have received. In this example we have just one new message, but you may have received multiple new messages:

You can recognize an unread message by the blue dot ● :

☞ **Tap the incoming message**

You will see the content of the message:

In the toolbar above a message you will find a few buttons. Here are the functions of these buttons:

Inbox (1)	View the content of the *Inbox* folder.
▲ ▼	Skip to the next or previous message.
⚑	Flag or mark a message as unread.
📁	Move a message to a different folder. The default folders include the *Inbox*, *Sent* and *Trash* folders.
🗑	Move a message to the *Trash* folder.
↩	Reply to a message, forward or print a message.
✎	Write a new message.

 Tip

Push or fetch

If you also retrieve your e-mail on a regular computer, you will be used to retrieving your e-mail through *fetch*: you open your e-mail program and it will connect to the mail server to retrieve your new messages. You can modify the program settings to check for new messages at regular intervals, while your e-mail program is open.

With the *push* function, new e-mail messages will be immediately sent to your e-mail program by the mail server, right after the mail server has received the messages. Even if your e-mail program has not been opened, and your iPad is locked.

The e-mail accounts from providers such as *Microsoft Exchange*, *MobileMe* and *Yahoo!* support push, but for other e-mail accounts, fetch is used.

Please note: if you connect to the Internet through the mobile data network and you do not have a contract for unlimited data transfer, it is recommended to turn off the push function. That is because you will be paying for the amount of data you use. If any e-mail messages with large attachments are pushed to your iPad, you might be facing higher data transfer fees. In this case, it is better to retrieve your e-mail manually, as soon as you have connected to the Internet through Wi-Fi.

- Continue on the next page -

This is how you can view the settings for push or fetch:

☞ **Open the *Settings* app** ✂⁶

👉 **Tap** [✉ Mail, Contacts, Calendars]

By default, [Push] is set for all e-mail accounts:

👉 **Tap**
   [Fetch New Data]

If you want to disable push:

👉 **Tap** [ON]

If push is disabled or is not supported by your provider, fetch will be used automatically. You can choose how often you want to retrieve new messages, or if you want to do that manually:

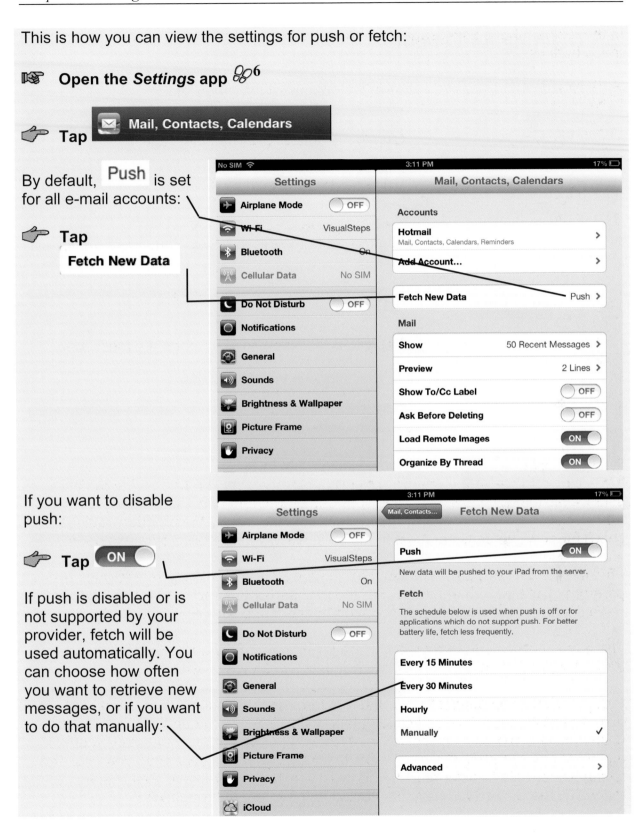

2.5 Deleting an E-mail

You are going to delete your test message:

👉 **Tap** 🗑

Now the e-mail message has been moved to the *Trash* folder. You can check to make sure:

👉 **Tap** `Inbox`

In this example there are no other messages in the *Inbox* folder:

If you have set up a single e-mail account:

👉 **Tap** `Mailboxes`

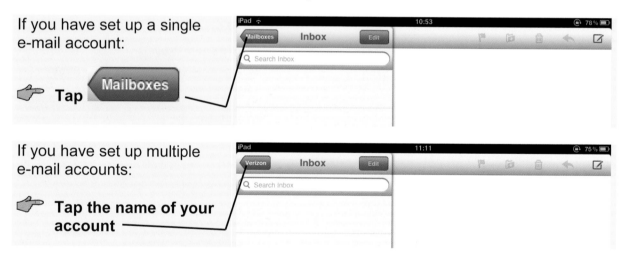

If you have set up multiple e-mail accounts:

👉 **Tap the name of your account**

You will see at least three folders:

👉 **Tap** 🗑 **Trash**

The deleted message is stored in the *Trash*:

This is how you permanently delete the message:

👉 **Tap the message**

You will see a red checkmark ✓ next to the message:

Now you can choose whether you want to delete the message or move it to another folder. You are going to delete the message:

👉 **Tap** Delete (1)

❔ Tip

Delete all messages

If you want to delete all messages, you do not need to tap the message. Instead:

☞ **Tap**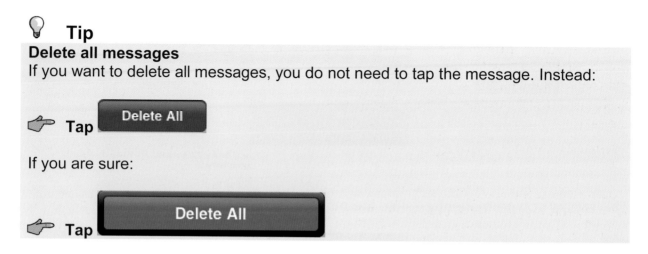

If you are sure:

☞ **Tap**

This is how you return to the *Inbox* if you have set up a single account:

☞ **Tap**

If you have set up multiple e-mail accounts:

☞ **Under Inboxes , tap the name of your account**

As soon as you open the *Inbox*, the program will automatically check for new messages. Down at the bottom, you will see the message

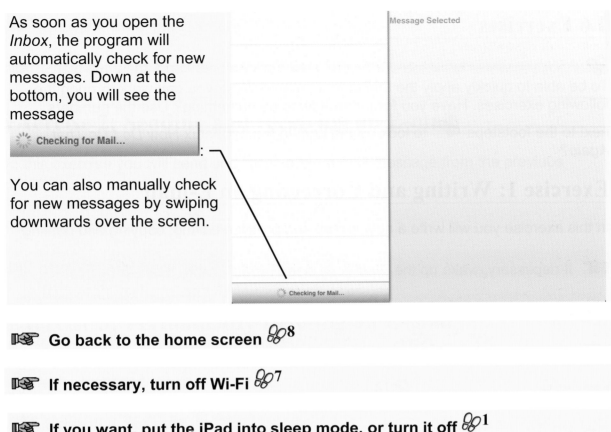

You can also manually check for new messages by swiping downwards over the screen.

☞ **Go back to the home screen** ⱽⱽ**⁸**

☞ **If necessary, turn off Wi-Fi** ⱽⱽ**⁷**

☞ **If you want, put the iPad into sleep mode, or turn it off** ⱽⱽ**¹**

💡 **Tip**

Multiple e-mail accounts
If you have set up more than one e-mail account on your iPad, the *Inbox* will look a bit different.

In this example, two e-mail accounts are used in the *Mail* app:

If you tap [All Inboxes] you will see all received messages from all two accounts:

In this chapter, you have set up an e-mail account on the iPad, sent and received an e-mail message and deleted an e-mail. In the following section you can practice these operations once more.

2.7 Background Information

Dictionary

Account	A combination of a user name and password that gives you access to a specific protected service. A subscription with an Internet service provider is also called an account.
AOL	Short for *America Online*, a major American Internet service provider.
Contacts	Standard app on the iPad with which you can view and edit the information about your contacts.
Fetch	Fetching is the traditional method of retrieving new e-mail messages: you open your e-mail program and connect with the mail server. You can set the program to check for e-mails at regular intervals, when the e-mail program is opened.
Gmail	Free e-mail service provided by the manufacturers of the well-known *Google* search engine.
Hotmail	Free e-mail service, part of *Windows Live Essentials*.
IMAP	IMAP stands for *Internet Message Access Protocol*. This means that you manage your e-mails on the mail server. Messages that you have read, will be stored on the mail server until you delete them. IMAP is useful if you want to manage your e-mail from multiple computers. Your mailbox will look the same on all the computers you use. If you create folders to organize your e-mail messages, these same folders will appear on each computer, as well as on your iPad. If you want to use IMAP, you will need to set up your e-mail account as an IMAP account on every computer you use.
Inbox	Folder in *Mail* where you can view the e-mail messages you have received.
Mail	Standard app on the iPad with which you can send and receive e-mail messages.

- Continue on the next page -

Microsoft Exchange	A mail server used by businesses, educational institutions and organizations.
Mobile Me	Paid online service by Apple, where users can synchronize their contacts, calendars and other items with a desktop or laptop computer, through the Internet and for a fixed annual fee.
Outlook	E-mail program that is part of the *Microsoft Office* suite.
POP	POP stands for *Post Office Protocol*, the traditional method of managing your e-mails. When you retrieve your e-mail, the messages will be deleted from the server right away. But on your iPad, the default setting for POP accounts is for saving a copy on the mail server, even after you have retrieved the message. This means you will also be able to retrieve the same message on your computer.
Push	When *push* is set and is supported by your provider, new e-mail messages will be sent to your e-mail program right after they are received on the mail server. Even when your e-mail program is not open and your iPad is locked.
Signature	Standard ending that will be inserted at the end of all your outgoing e-mails.
Synchronize	Literally this means: making things the same. Not only can you synchronize your iPad with the content of your *iTunes Library*, but you can also synchronize the data of an e-mail account.
Trash	Folder in *Mail* where all your deleted messages are stored. Once you have deleted a message from the *Trash*, it will be deleted permanently.
Yahoo!	Search engine that also offers free e-mail services.

Source: User Guide iPad, Wikipedia.

2.8 Tips

 Tip

Formatting text in an e-mail message

You can format the text in an e-mail message. You can underline specific words, or render them in bold or italic letters. This is how you render a word in bold:

☞ **Select a word** �[19]

👉 **Tap** `B I U`

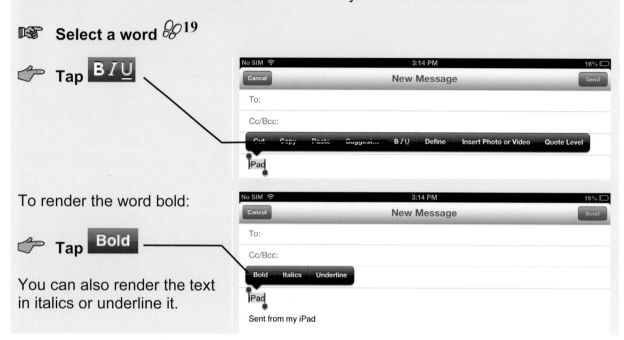

To render the word bold:

👉 **Tap** `Bold`

You can also render the text in italics or underline it.

 Tip

Disable Auto-Correction

Sometimes, the autocorrect function on the iPad will insert unwanted corrections. The dictionary will not recognize every single word you type, but will try to suggest a correction, nevertheless. This may result in strange corrections, which you might accept without knowing it, whenever you type a period, comma or blank space. This is how to disable the autocorrect function:

☞ **Open the *Settings* app** ⍽[6]

👉 **At the bottom, tap**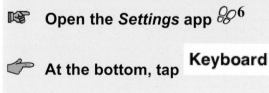

- Continue on the next page -

☞ **By** Auto-Correction **, tap the** ON **button**

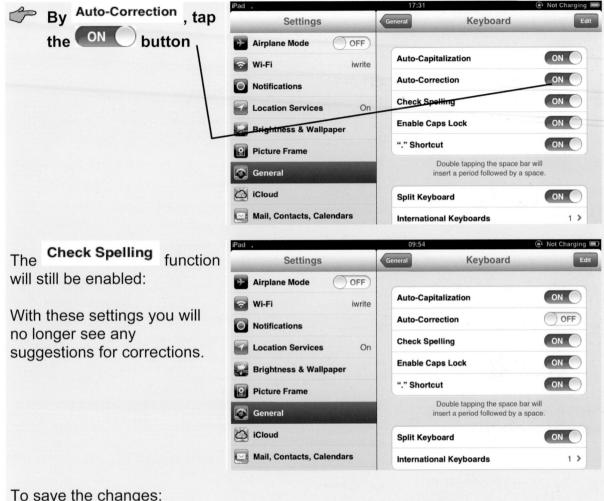

The Check Spelling function will still be enabled:

With these settings you will no longer see any suggestions for corrections.

To save the changes:

 Press the Home button and return to your home screen 🐾**8**

💡 **Tip**

Signature

By default, each e-mail you send will end with the text *Sent from my iPad*. This text is called your *signature*. You can replace this text by a standard ending for your messages or by your name and address. This is how to change your e-mail signature:

 Open the *Settings* app 🐾**6**

- Continue on the next page -

☞ **Tap**

✉ **Mail, Contacts, Calenc**

☞ **Tap** **Signature**

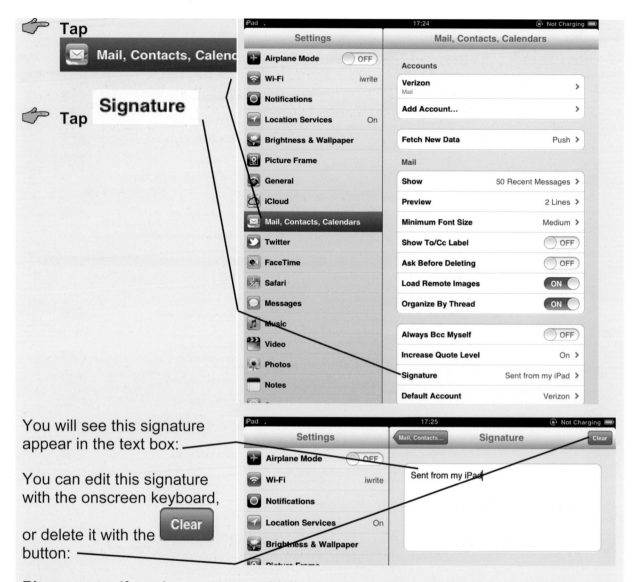

You will see this signature appear in the text box:

You can edit this signature with the onscreen keyboard,

or delete it with the **Clear** button:

Please note: if you have set up multiple e-mail accounts, this signature will be used for all the messages that are sent from these accounts.

 Tip

iPad horizontal

If you hold the iPad in a horizontal position, by default, you will see your mailbox with e-mail messages on your screen:

The mailbox with the messages:

The e-mail message:

Tip

Should I save my e-mails on the server or not?

For POP e-mail accounts you can modify the settings yourself and choose to save a copy of the received e-mails on the mail server. If a copy is stored, you will also be able to retrieve the e-mail messages on your computer, even after you have retrieved them on your iPad. Here is how to modify the settings to suit your own preferences:

☞ **Open the *Settings* app**
$\mathscr{C}\mathscr{C}$6

☞ **Tap**
✉ Mail, Contacts, Calendars

☞ **Tap your POP e-mail account**

You will see the page with the account information. At this point, you may want to hide the onscreen keyboard:

☞ **At the bottom right, tap** ⌨▾

☞ **Tap** **Advanced**

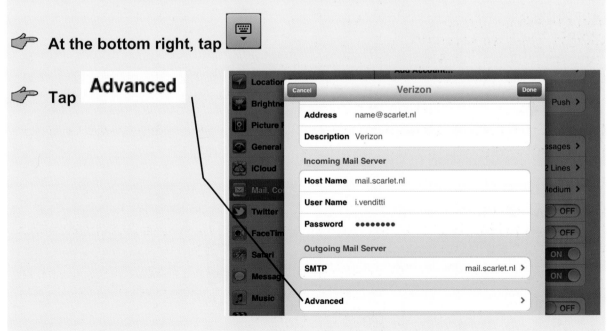

- Continue on the next page -

By default, the setting is for new e-mails never to be deleted from the server. This means that the messages will only be deleted from the server if you retrieve them in an e-mail program where the setting is adjusted in such a way that the messages from the server will be deleted.

☞ **Tap**

You can set the program never to delete messages from the mail server, delete them after seven days, or only after they have been deleted from the *Inbox* folder:

☞ **Tap the desired option**

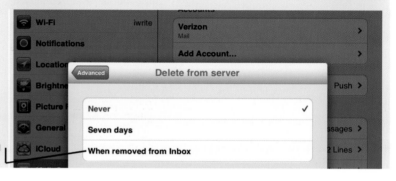

💡 **Tip**

Synchronize from Outlook

If you use the *Microsoft Outlook (Express)* e-mail program on your computer, you can also synchronize the data of your e-mail account with your iPad. Actually, this is pretty much the same thing as you learned above in *section 2.1 Setting Up an E-mail Account*. Your messages will not be moved. Your account settings will be adjusted.

👉 **Connect your iPad to the computer**

👉 **By DEVICES, click your iPad, for instance**
🗖 Studio Visual...

The *Summary* tab will be opened:

👉 **Click the Info tab**

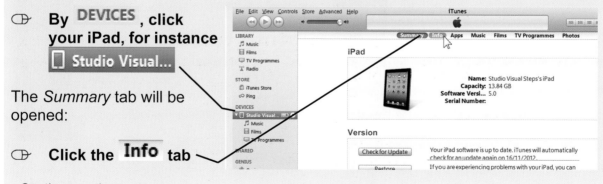

- Continue on the next page -

With the *Info* tab you can synchronize all sorts of data with your iPad:

☞ **Drag the scroll bar downwards**

☞ **Check the box ☑ at Sync Mail Accounts fi**

Outlook is automatically selected:

☞ **Check the box ☑ next to the e-mail account(s) you want to synchronize**

Now you can start the synchronization:

☞ **Click** Apply

In the top of the window you will see a progress bar:

Now the data of your e-mail account have been synchronized.

For security reasons, the passwords are not synchronized. You will need to enter these on your iPad:

☞ **Safely disconnect the iPad from the computer** $\mathcal{B}^9$

☞ **Wake up the iPad from sleep mode** $\mathcal{B}^2$

☞ **If necessary, turn on Wi-Fi** $\mathcal{B}^{10}$

☞ **Tap**

✉ **Mail, Contacts, Calendars**

☞ **Tap your e-mail account**

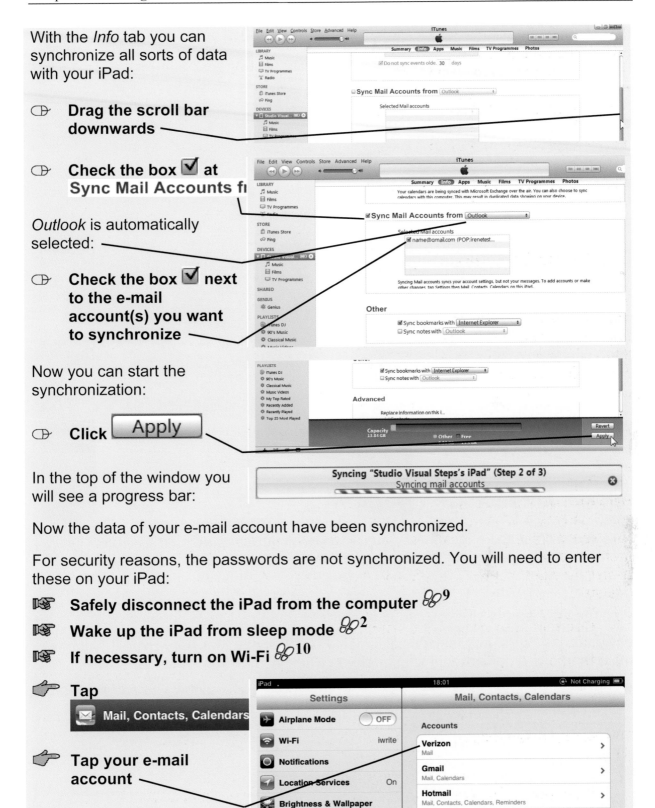

- Continue on the next page -

By default, your e-mail address is entered in the **Description** field: you can also type a different, identifiable name for your e-mail account.

Now add your password:

👉 Tap **Password**

⌨ **Type your password with the onscreen keyboard**

👉 Tap **Done**

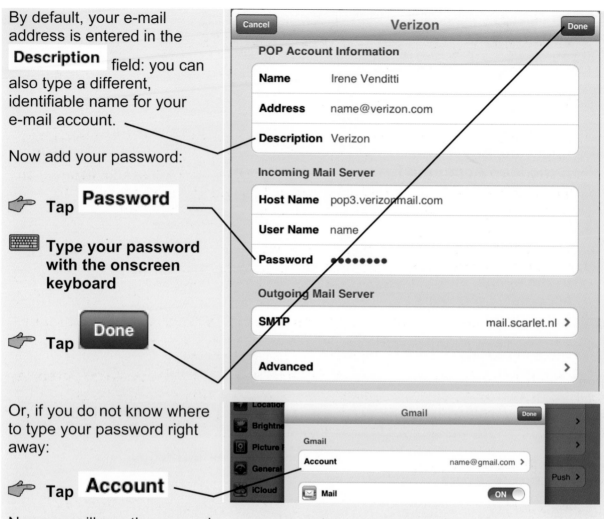

Or, if you do not know where to type your password right away:

👉 Tap **Account**

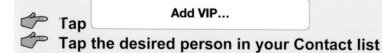

Now you will see the page where you can enter your password.

 Tip

VIP

With the new feature VIP you can automatically route mail from persons you designate as "VIPs" into the special folder ⭐ **VIP** in the Mail app. Even if you have more than one email account set up for you iPad, all mail from your "VIPs" will automatically appear in the ⭐ **VIP** folder (mailbox). Here is how you add someone to the VIP list.

👉 Tap   **Add VIP...**

👉 **Tap the desired person in your Contact list**

In *Chapter 4 The Standard Apps on your iPad* you will learn how to add new people to the list in the Contacts app.

3. Surfing with Your iPad

In this chapter you are going to get acquainted with *Safari*, the web browser used by all Apple devices. With this web browser you can surf the Internet using your iPad. If you are familiar with using the Internet on your computer, you will see that surfing on the iPad is just as easy. The big difference is that you do not need a mouse, or keyboard to navigate. You surf by using the touchscreen on your iPad.

You will learn how to open a web page, zoom in and out and how to scroll by touching the screen in a specific way. We will also discuss how to open a link (or hyperlink) and work with web pages that you have saved, also called bookmarks.

In *Safari* you can open up to nine web pages at a time. In this chapter you will learn how to switch back and forth between these open pages.

While you are surfing, you may want to do something else, such as listening to some music or modifying a particular setting. Your iPad can perform multiple tasks simultaneously, so this is not a problem. You can switch from one app to another app easily. In this chapter you will learn how to do this.

In this chapter you will learn how to:

- open *Safari*;
- open a web page;
- zoom in and zoom out;
- scroll;
- open a link on a new tab;
- switch between multiple open page tabs
- add a bookmark;
- search;
- switch between recently used apps;
- view the settings of *Safari*;
- use a different search engine.

3.1 Opening Safari

This is how you open *Safari*, the app that allows you to surf the Internet:

☞ **Wake up the iPad from sleep mode or turn it on** $\mathscr{O}^2$

☞ **If necessary, turn on Wi-Fi** $\mathscr{O}^{10}$

☞ Tap

If you have not used *Safari* before, this page will be blank:

3.2 Opening a Web Page

This is to how to display the onscreen keyboard, in order to enter the web address:

☞ **Tap the address bar**

To practice, you can take a look at the Visual Steps website:

⌨ **Type:**
www.visualsteps
.com

When you have finished typing:

☞ **Tap** Go

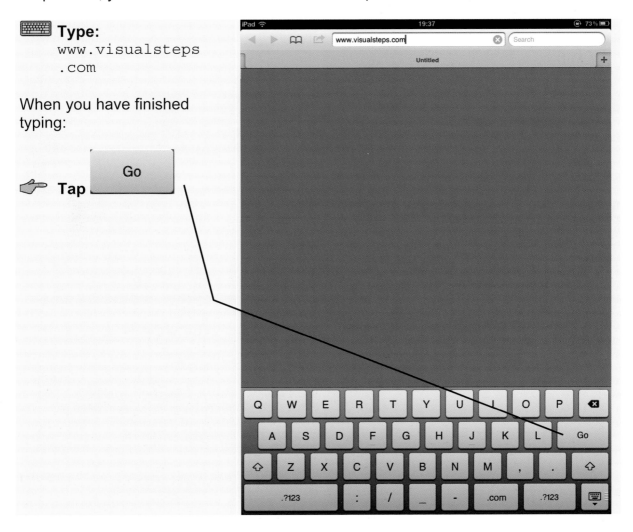

HELP! A web address is already entered.

If another web address is shown in the address bar, you can delete it like this:

 Tap ⊗

Now you will see the Visual
Steps website:

3.3 Zoom In and Zoom Out

If you think that the letters and images on a website are too small, you can zoom in.
This is done by double-tapping. Tap the desired spot twice, in rapid succession:

☞ **Double-tap the menu**
on the left-hand side

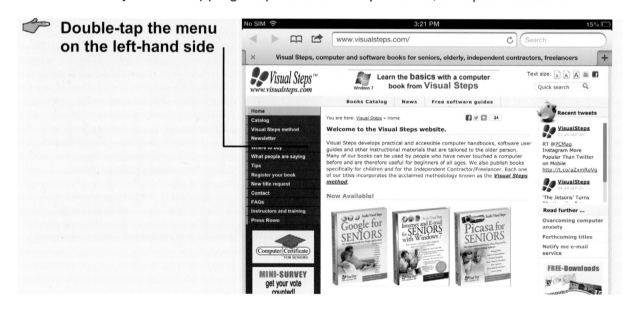

HELP! A new web page is opened.

If you do not double-tap in the right way, a new tab might be opened. If that is the case, just tap ◀ on the screen at the top left and try again. You can also practice double-tapping in a blank area of your screen.

You will see that the web page is rendered in a larger size:

☞ **Double-tap the menu once more**

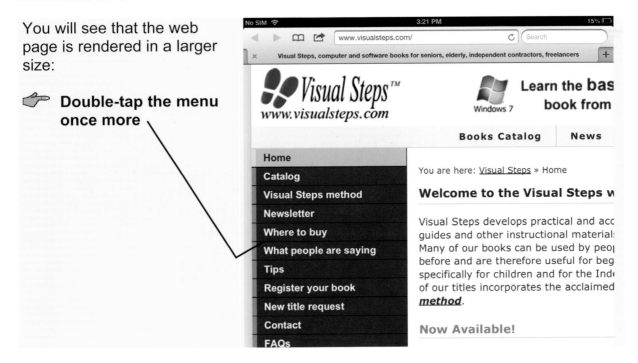

Now the screen will zoom out to the standard view again. There is also another way to zoom in and out; sort of like pinching. You use your thumb and index finger. Set them on the spot that you want to enlarge:

☞ **Slowly spread your thumb and index finger away from each other on the screen**

You will see that you can zoom in even further. It will take a moment for the screen to focus. You can zoom out by reversing the movement of your fingers:

Move your thumb and index finger towards each other on the screen

Now you are going to return to the view you had when you zoomed in for the first time:

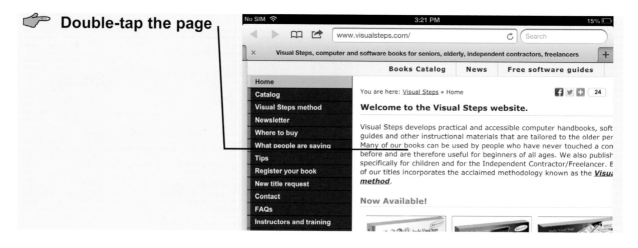

Double-tap the page

You will see the view after zooming in once:

3.4 Scrolling

Scrolling allows you to view the entire content of the web page. You scroll up or down to see more of the page. On your iPad, you do this with your fingers:

👉 **Drag your finger upwards a bit, on the screen**

You will see that the page scrolls downwards:

👉 **Drag your finger downwards a bit, on the screen**

You will see that the page scrolls upwards:

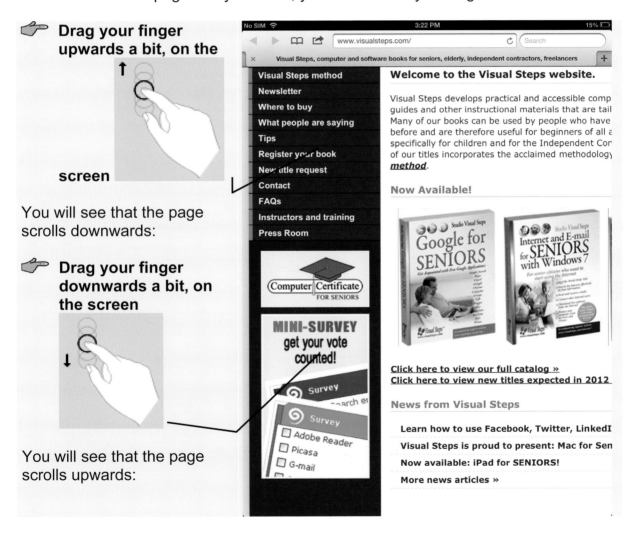

Tip

Scrolling sideways
You can scroll sideways by moving your finger from right to left, or from left to right.

If you want to quickly scroll a longer page, you can swipe your finger over the screen:

 Move your finger upwards in a swiping gesture, over the screen

You will see that you will quickly scroll down to the bottom of the page:

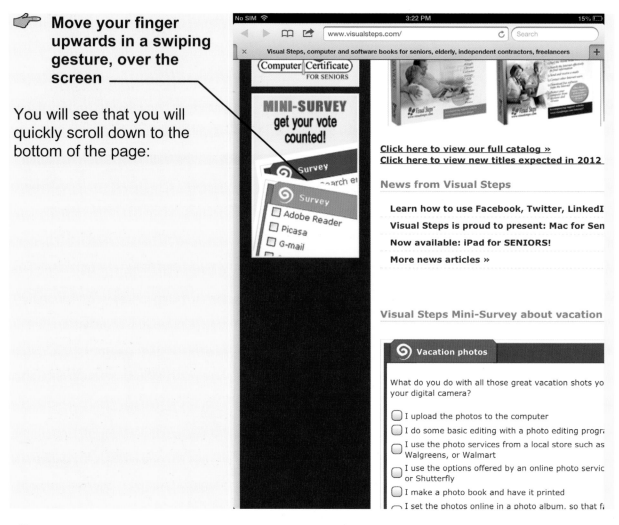

  Tip

Moving in different directions
You can also quickly scroll upwards, to the left, or to the right, if you swipe the screen in that direction.

This is how you quickly return to the top of the web page:

☞ **Tap the black status bar**

At once, you will jump to the top of the web page:

3.5 Opening a Link on a Web Page

If a page contains a (hyper) link, you can follow this link by tapping it. Just try this:

☞ Tap **Catalog**

✛ **HELP! Tapping the link does not work.**

If you find it difficult to tap the right link, you can zoom in first. This way, the links will be displayed in a much larger format, and tapping the link will be easier.

Now the catalog will be opened, where you can view the Visual Steps books:

Here you see that the new page is displayed in the regular size:

3.6 Opening a Link in a New Tab

You can also open a link in a new tab:

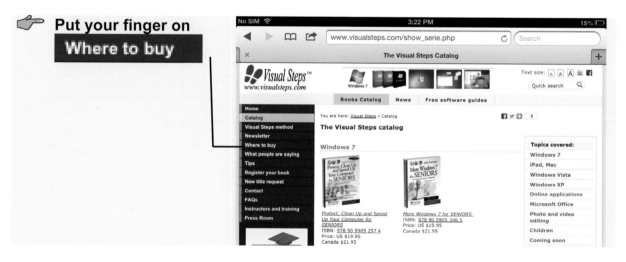

☞ **Put your finger on**
Where to buy

In a few seconds, you will see a menu:

👉 **Tap**

Open in New Tab

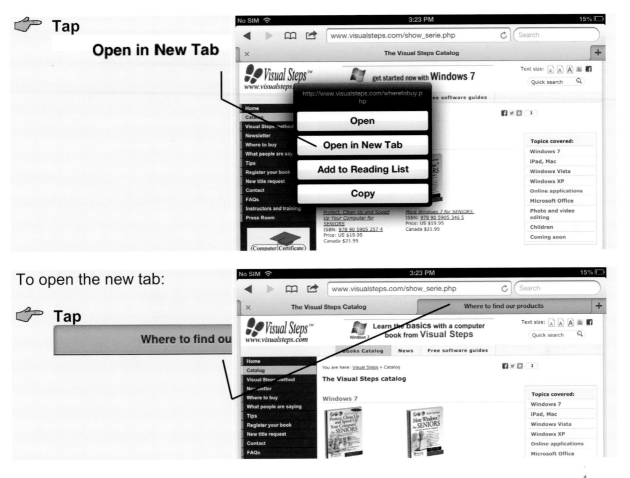

To open the new tab:

👉 **Tap**

Where to find ou

Now you will see the information on where to find the Visual Steps products:

You can sign up for our *Notify me* e-mail service. Then you will be notified by e-mail when each new book is released. You can open this page on a new tab:

👉 **Put your finger on**

Notify me e-mail service

In a few seconds, you will see a menu:

☞ **Tap**

Open in New Tab

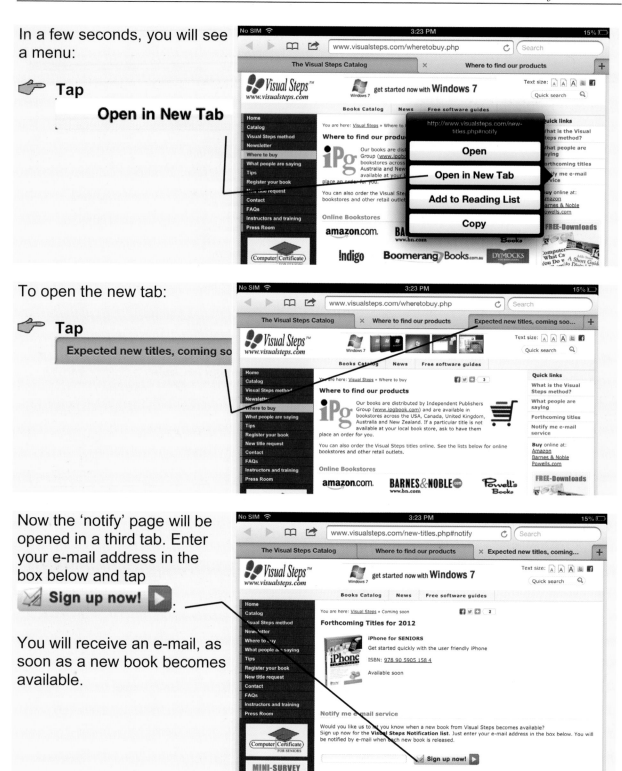

To open the new tab:

☞ **Tap**

Expected new titles, coming so

Now the 'notify' page will be opened in a third tab. Enter your e-mail address in the box below and tap

✉ **Sign up now!** ▶ :

You will receive an e-mail, as soon as a new book becomes available.

3.7 Switching Between Multiple Tabs

A very useful option in *Safari* is being able to switch between a maximum of nine tabs with open web pages.

At the top of the page you will see three tabs:

This means that at the moment, three web pages are opened. This is how you return to the second page:

☞ **Tap** | **Where to find our products**

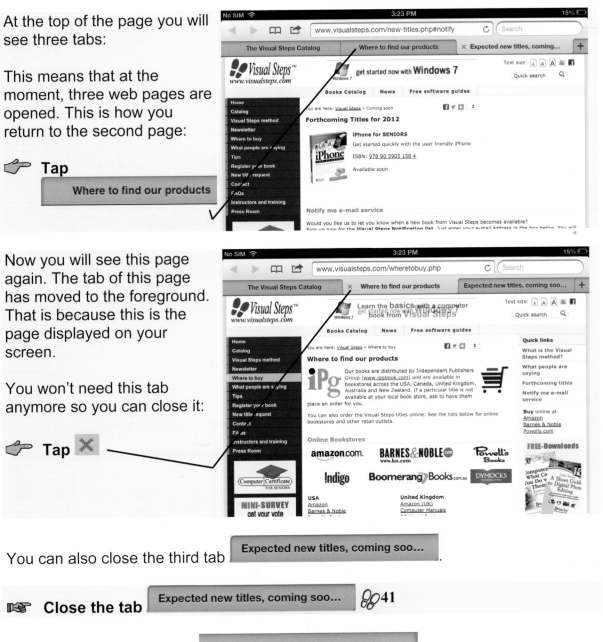

Now you will see this page again. The tab of this page has moved to the foreground. That is because this is the page displayed on your screen.

You won't need this tab anymore so you can close it:

☞ **Tap** ✖

You can also close the third tab **Expected new titles, coming soo…** .

☞ **Close the tab** **Expected new titles, coming soo…** 🐾**41**

In this example the first tab **The Visual Steps Catalog** will be left open. But if you close all open tabs, you will again see the blank page you saw at the beginning of this chapter.

Tip
Enter a new web address in the address bar
If you want to type a new address in the address bar, you can remove the web address of the open web page in the following way:

 Tap the address bar

 Tap ⊗

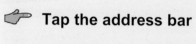 **Tip**
Open a new, blank page in a new tab
This is how you open a new, blank page in *Safari*:

☞ **Tap** ➕

You will see a new, untitled tab:

The onscreen keyboard will be opened. Now you can enter a new keyword in the *Google* search box.

3.8 Go to Previous or to Next Page

You can return to the web page you have previously visited. Here is how to do that:

☞ **Tap** ◀

You will again see the Visual Steps home page. You can also skip to the next page. To do this, you use the ▶ button, but right now this will not be necessary.

3.9 Creating a Reading List

In *Safari* you can create a reading list. A *reading list* contains links to web pages you want to visit at a later time. This is how you add the current page to a reading list:

☞ **Tap**

☞ **Tap** Add to Reading List

The page will be added to the reading list.

You can also add a link to the reading list like this:

☞ **Put your finger on** Catalog

Wait a moment for the menu to appear:

☞ **Tap**

Add to Reading List

You can view the contents of the reading list:

☞ **Tap**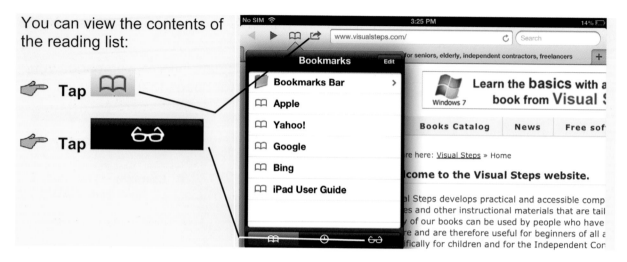

☞ **Tap**

To open a web page you have previously saved:

☞ **Tap**
   Catalog
   visualsteps.com
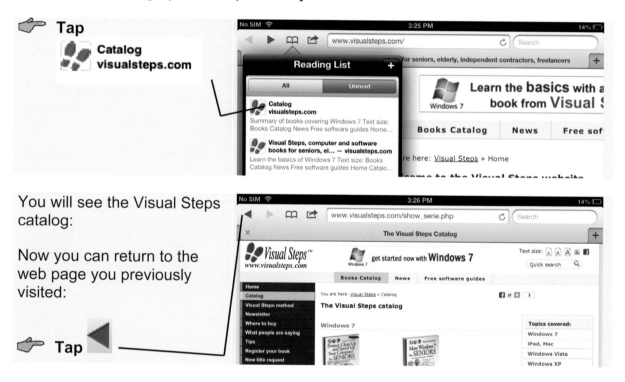

You will see the Visual Steps catalog:

Now you can return to the web page you previously visited:

☞ **Tap**

The page has been read and will be removed from the reading list.

3.10 Adding a Bookmark

If you want to visit a page more often, you can make a bookmark for this page. A bookmark is a favorite website which you want to visit again, later on. In this way, you do not need to type the full web address every time you want to visit the site.

A bookmark will be saved in *Safari* even after you have viewed the web page. This is how you add a bookmark:

👉 **Tap**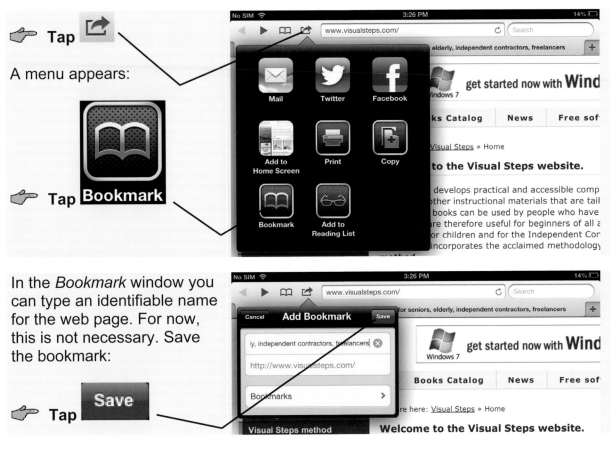

A menu appears:

👉 **Tap Bookmark**

In the *Bookmark* window you can type an identifiable name for the web page. For now, this is not necessary. Save the bookmark:

👉 **Tap Save**

The web page has been added to your bookmarks. You can check this yourself:

👉 **Tap**

👉 **Tap**

You will see the new
bookmark in the list: —

Apple has added a number of
useful bookmarks to this list,
such as an iPad User Guide:

This is how you open the
Visual Steps bookmark:

☞ **Tap**

    📖 **Visual Steps, computer**

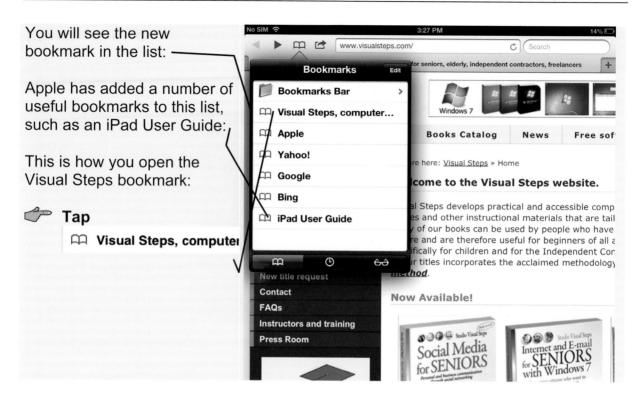

Now the Visual Steps web page will be opened.

3.11 Searching

In *Safari*, *Google* is set as the default search engine. You can use the search box in
the same way as in other Internet browsers, which you may already have used on
your computer. This is how to start a search:

☞ **Tap**

    Search

The search box will become larger and the onscreen keyboard is displayed. Now you can type your keyword(s):

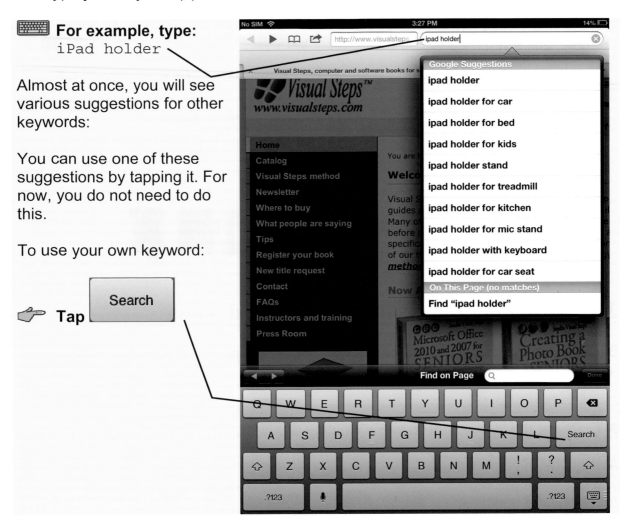

For example, type:
iPad holder

Almost at once, you will see various suggestions for other keywords:

You can use one of these suggestions by tapping it. For now, you do not need to do this.

To use your own keyword:

Tap **Search**

Exercise 3: Open a Link

In this exercise you are going to use different methods for following a link to an interesting article on a new page.

☞ Open a link to an interesting article. $\mathscr{C}^{38}$

☞ If possible, scroll downwards to the end of the article. $\mathscr{C}^{31}$

☞ Open a link to another article in a new tab. $\mathscr{C}^{39}$

☞ Open the page on the other tab. $\mathscr{C}^{40}$

Exercise 4: Recently Used Apps

In this exercise you are going to switch between recently used apps.

☞ Take a look at the recently used apps. $\mathscr{C}^{42}$

☞ Switch to the *Settings* app. $\mathscr{C}^{43}$

☞ Take a look at the recently used apps. $\mathscr{C}^{42}$

☞ Open the *Safari* app. $\mathscr{C}^{29}$

☞ If necessary, turn off Wi-Fi. $\mathscr{C}^{7}$

☞ If you want, put the iPad into sleep mode or turn it off. $\mathscr{C}^{1}$

3.14 Background Information

Dictionary

Bing	Search engine manufactured by *Microsoft*.
Bookmark	A link to a web address that has been stored in a list, so you can easily find the web page later on.
Google	Search engine.
Hyperlink	A hyperlink is a navigation tool on a web page, which will automatically lead the user to the information when it is tapped. A hyperlink can be displayed in text or in an image, such as a photo, a button or an icon. Also called link.
Link	A different name for a hyperlink.
Safari	Web browser manufactured by Apple.
Scroll	Moving a web page on the screen upwards, downwards, to the left, or to the right. To do this on the iPad you need to touch the screen in a certain way.
Yahoo!	Search engine.
Zoom in	Take a closer look at an item; the letters and images will become larger.
Zoom out	Look at an item from a distance; the letters and images will become smaller.

Source: iPad User Guide, Wikipedia

Flash
The fact that your iPad cannot display *Flash* content is a bit of a limitation. *Flash* is a technique that is used for interactive websites and animations on websites. As a result of this, some elements of a web page may not be correctly rendered on the iPad.

3.15 Tips

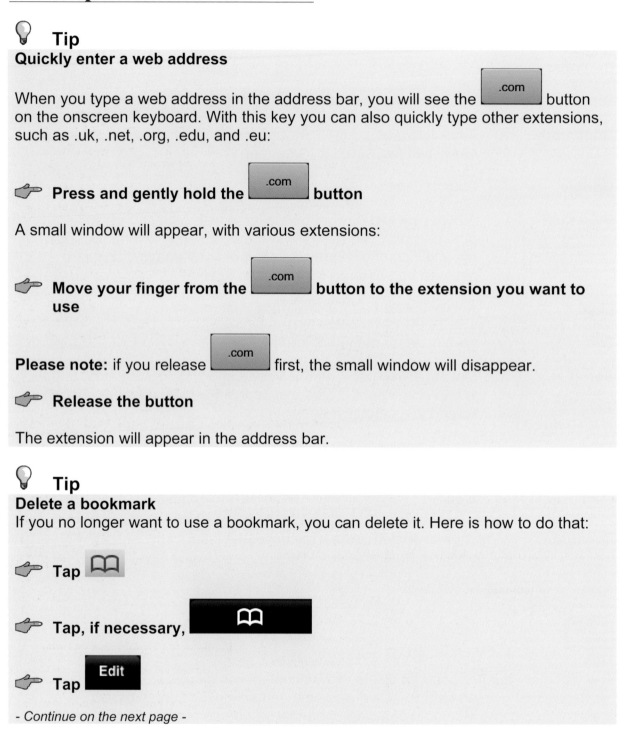

Tip

Quickly enter a web address

When you type a web address in the address bar, you will see the .com button on the onscreen keyboard. With this key you can also quickly type other extensions, such as .uk, .net, .org, .edu, and .eu:

☞ **Press and gently hold the** .com **button**

A small window will appear, with various extensions:

☞ **Move your finger from the** .com **button to the extension you want to use**

Please note: if you release .com first, the small window will disappear.

☞ **Release the button**

The extension will appear in the address bar.

Tip

Delete a bookmark

If you no longer want to use a bookmark, you can delete it. Here is how to do that:

☞ Tap 📖

☞ Tap, if necessary, 📖

☞ Tap **Edit**

- Continue on the next page -

Tap 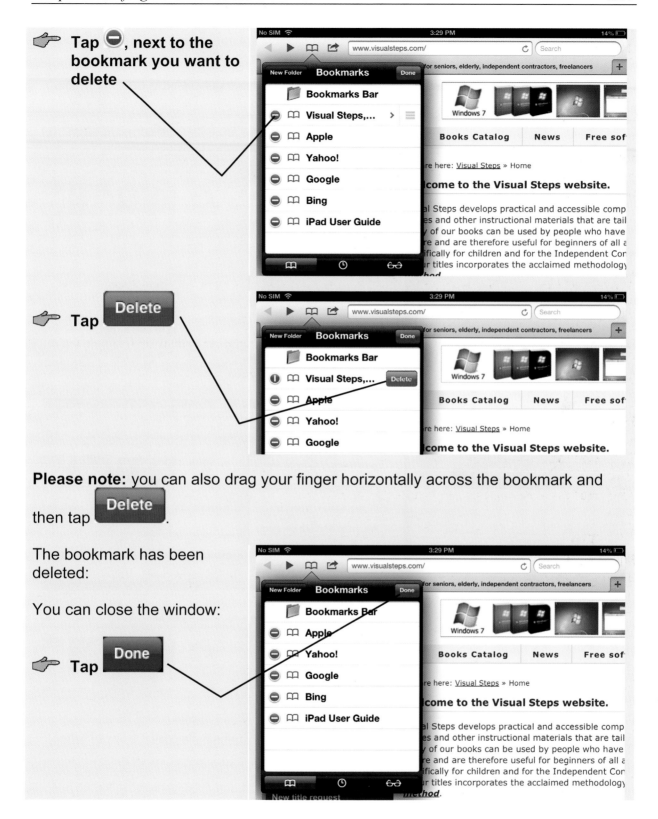, next to the bookmark you want to delete

Tap **Delete**

Please note: you can also drag your finger horizontally across the bookmark and then tap **Delete**.

The bookmark has been deleted:

You can close the window:

Tap **Done**

Tip

View and delete history
In the history, all recently visited websites are stored. This is how you can view the history:

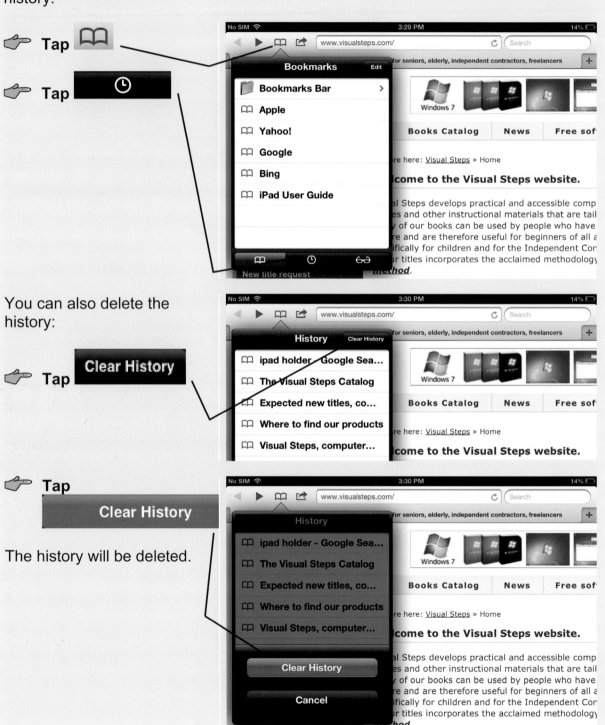

☞ Tap 📖

☞ Tap 🕐

You can also delete the history:

☞ Tap **Clear History**

☞ Tap **Clear History**

The history will be deleted.

💡 Tip

Synchronize bookmarks with Internet Explorer or Safari

If you have stored lots of favorites (bookmarks) on your computer, in *Internet Explorer* or *Safari*, you can synchronize these with your iPad.

☞ **Connect your iPad to the computer**

The *iTunes* program will automatically open.

↪ **By** DEVICES **, click your iPad, for instance,** 🔲 Studio Visual

↪ **Click the** Info **tab**

↪ **Drag the scroll bar downwards**

↪ **By** Other **, check the box** ☑️ **at** Sync bookmarks with

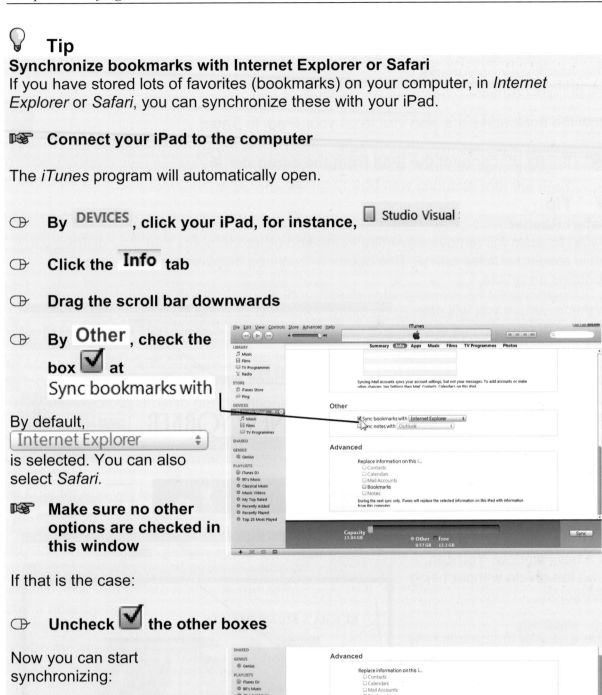

By default, Internet Explorer ⬍ is selected. You can also select *Safari*.

☞ **Make sure no other options are checked in this window**

If that is the case:

↪ **Uncheck** ☑️ **the other boxes**

Now you can start synchronizing:

↪ **Click** Apply

- Continue on the next page -

4.1 Adding a Contact

You can open the *Contacts* app on the home screen of your iPad.

☞ **Wake the iPad up from sleep or turn it on** 👣²

👉 **Tap** **Contacts**

In this example we do not have any contacts yet. You can add a new contact like this:

👉 **Tap** **+**

You can practice with a fictitious contact or if you like, use a real person that you know. You will be using the onscreen keyboard:

Type the first name of your contact

Tap Last

Type the last name of your contact

Tap Phone

Type the cell phone number of your contact

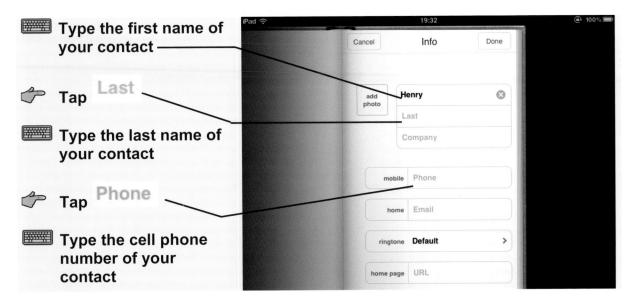

Please note:

When you enter a phone number, the digits will automatically be grouped in the right order, including parentheses, dashes or no dashes as needed. The format used depends on the region format settings in the *Settings* app.

As soon as you start entering a phone number in the **mobile** field, a new line will appear where you can enter another phone number. This will also happen when you enter data in other fields. The default label for the second phone number field is **home**. You can change the name of this label and other labels as well. You can call the label for the next number home or work, for example:

Tap home

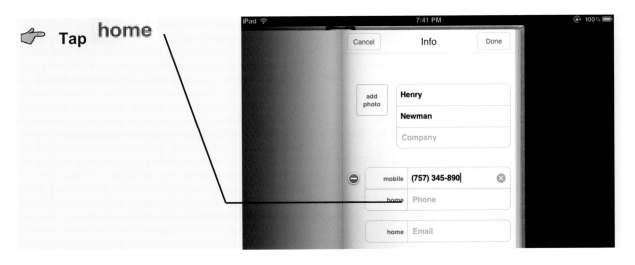

You will see a list from which you can select a label:

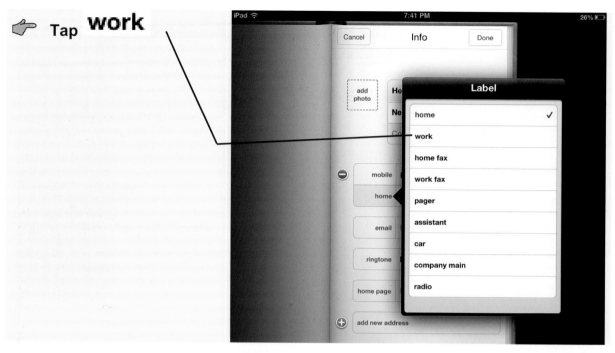

👉 Tap **work**

⌨ **Type your contact's home number**

You will see that again, a new field appears for entering a third phone number:

You do not need to enter another number now.

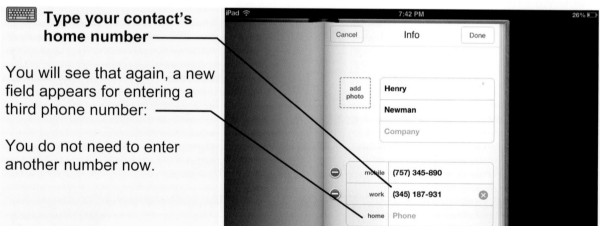

You can enter a lot of other information about your contact. It is up to you to fill in all the fields, or leave them blank.

👉 **Add your contact's e-mail address. If he or she has a homepage (web address) you can enter that as well.** 👣44

Tip

Change the label
You can change the label for the e-mail address. You can select "home" for a personal e-mail address and "work" for a work-related one, for example.

At the bottom of the page you will find even more fields:

👉 **Drag the page upwards**

👉 **Tap**
add new address

Now you can add the physical address

⌨ **Type the street name and house number**

At once, you will see a second new line for street information:

You do not need this now.

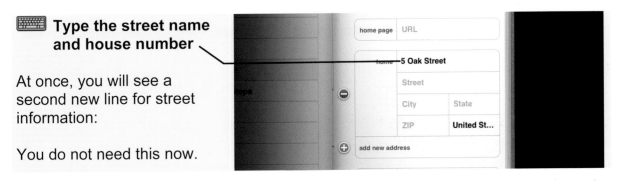

☞ **Add your contact's zip code, postal code, city name, county or state name**

Now you can save your contact:

Now your contact will appear in the **All Contacts** list:

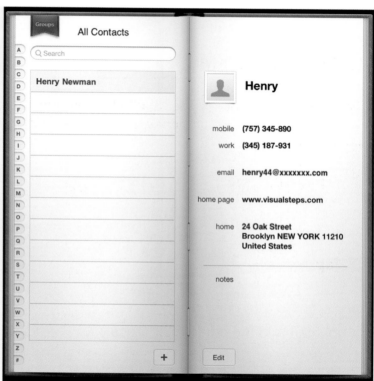

 Add another four contacts ℰℰ⁴⁵

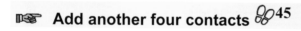 **Tip**

Add a field for a middle name

A contact called De Vere will be listed under the letter D in the *All Contacts* list. If you prefer to classify this name under the letter V, you can add a field for the middle name:

👉 **Drag the page all the way upwards**

👉 **Tap**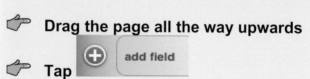

- Continue on the next page -

You will see a list of fields you can add:

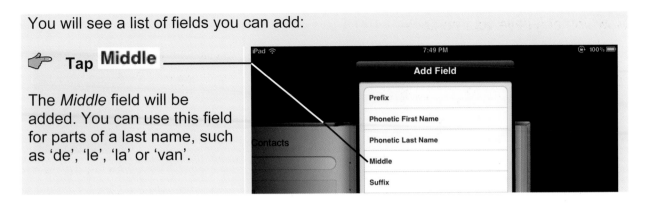

☞ **Tap** **Middle**

The *Middle* field will be added. You can use this field for parts of a last name, such as 'de', 'le', 'la' or 'van'.

4.2 Editing a Contact

After you have entered all your contacts, you might want to edit them. Perhaps, a contact has moved and has a new address or a new phone number. This is how you open a contact for editing:

☞ **Tap the desired contact**

☞ **Tap** Edit

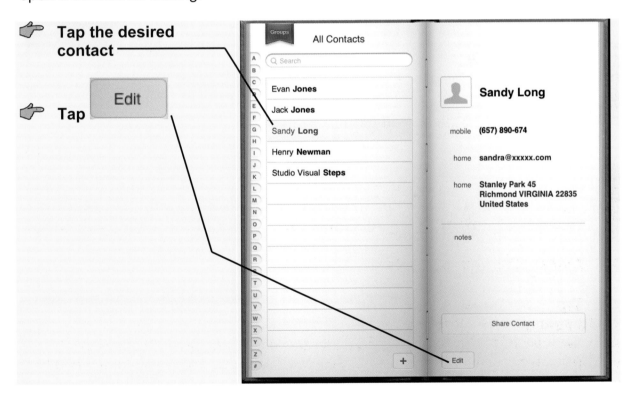

If you need to change the phone number:

☞ **Tap the phone number**

☞ **Tap** ✕

The phone number will be deleted:

⌨ **Type the new phone number** ───

☞ **Tap** | Done |

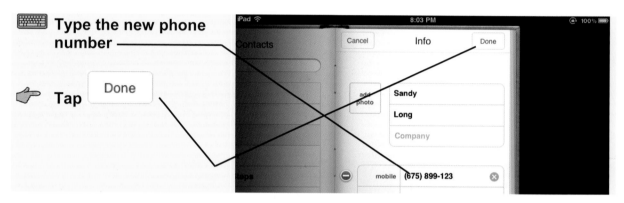

You can do the same thing for any other field that needs editing.

☞ **Return to the home screen** 👣8

💡 **Tip**

Delete a field

If you want to delete a particular field from the contact information, you do not need to open the relevant contact. In the All Contacts list:

☞ **Tap the desired contact**

☞ **Drag your finger across the field you want to delete** ───

☞ **Tap** | Delete |

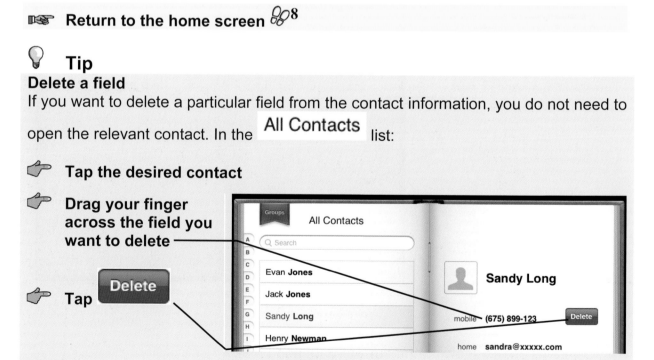

Please note: you can also use this same action in many other apps.

Tip
Delete a contact
This is how to delete someone from your contact list:

☞   **Tap the desired contact**

☞   **Tap** Edit

☞   **Drag the page upwards**

☞   **Tap**
Delete Contact

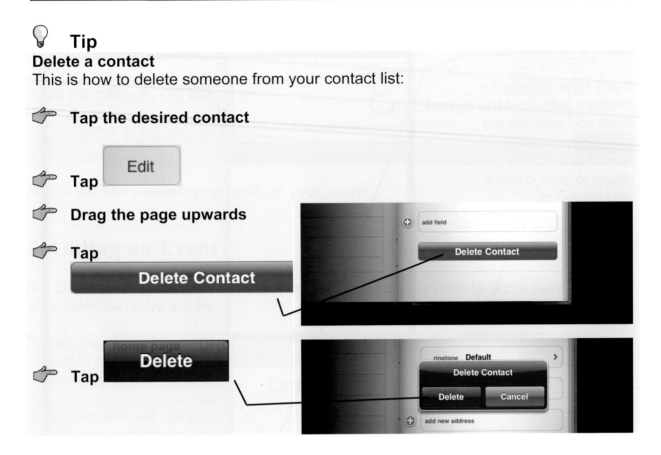

☞   **Tap** **Delete**

4.3 Calendar

With the *Calendar* app you can keep track of your appointments, upcoming activities, birthdays and more. You open the *Calendar* app like this:

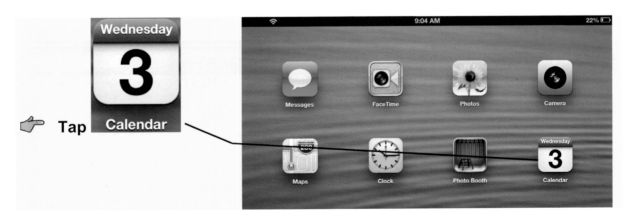

☞   **Tap** Calendar

The calendar opens showing the current date and time.

You can also add an event by pressing your finger on the calendar screen. You do that like this:

☞ **Press your finger on the desired date and time**

You will see a menu:

☞ **Enter the necessary data**

☞ **Tap** Done

Now the event has been added to the calendar:

💡 **Tip**

Edit or delete an event

When a certain event changes or is canceled, you can edit it or delete it:

☞ **Tap the event**

☞ **Tap** Edit

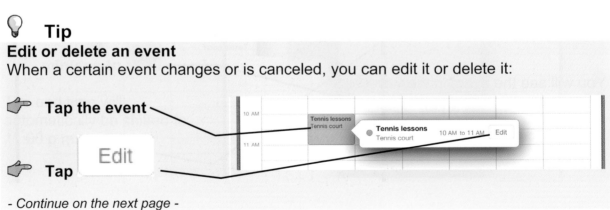

- Continue on the next page -

In this screen you can change the description, location, date, or time of the event. When you have finished:

☞ **Tap** Done

If you want to delete the event:

☞ **Tap**

Delete Event

You need to confirm this:

☞ **Tap**

Delete Event

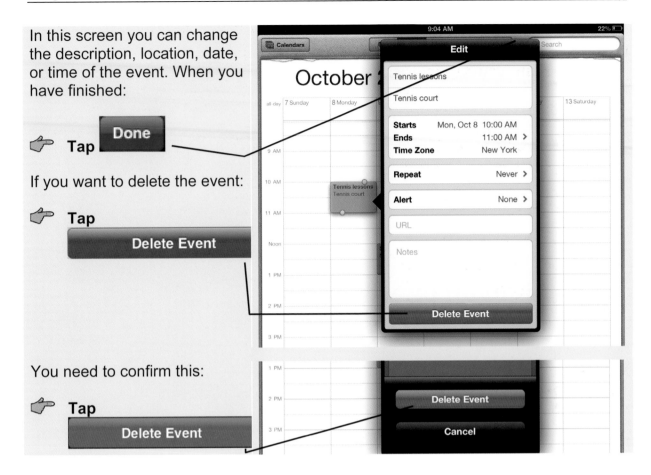

4.5 Notes

Notes is a handy app for writing text quickly. You have worked briefly with this app in *Chapter 1 The iPad.* You can jot down a few thoughts, make a grocery or a to-do list, or a list of things to remember when you go on holiday, even copy and paste a recipe from a website. You can open this app like this:

☞ **Go back to the home screen** 👣[8]

☞ **Tap** Notes

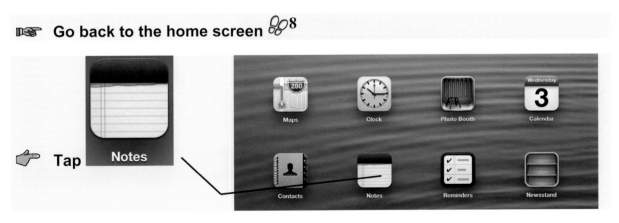

You will see a new, blank notes page:

👉 **Tap the first line**

⌨ **Type:** Holiday

return

👉 **Tap twice**

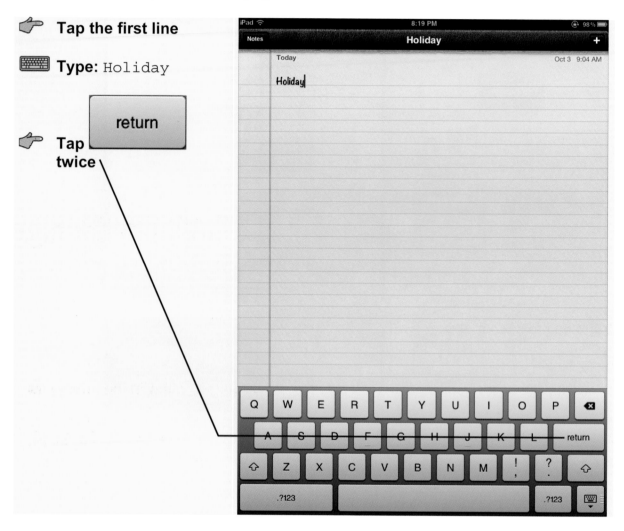

You can make a simple list:

⌨ **Type this list:**

Holiday

Renew passport
Change currency
Shots?
Get travel insurance!

You can edit multiple notes at once. This is how you open a new note:

👉 **Tap** **+**

You can make a grocery list:

This is how you can see which notes are opened:

Two notes have been opened. This is how to go back to the note with the holiday list:

💡 **Tip**

Flip through the opened notes

At the bottom of the notes page you will see various buttons. You can use one of these buttons to skip to the next note:

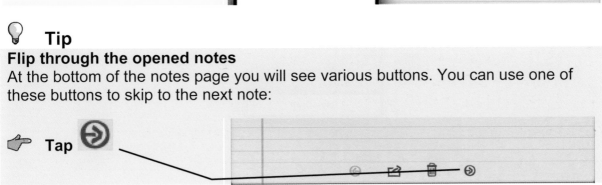

You will see the *Holiday* note again. You can quickly send this note by e-mail:

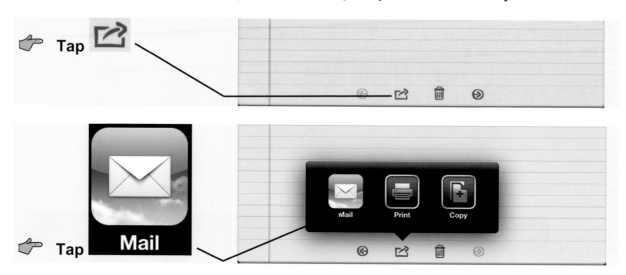

A new e-mail message will be opened, containing the text of the note. If you want to send the e-mail, you can do this in the same way you learned in *Chapter 2 Sending E-mails with Your iPad*. For now, you do not need to send this e-mail:

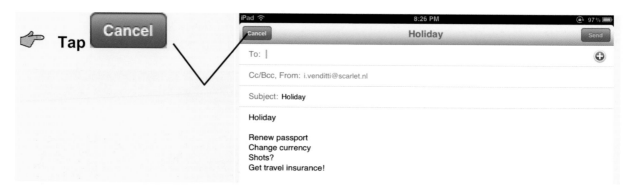

You do not need to save the draft:

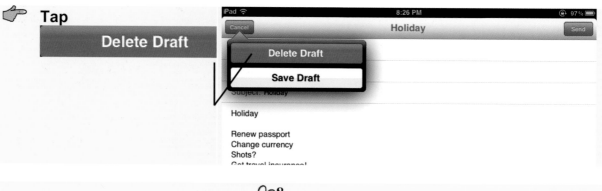

☞ **Go back to the home screen** 👣⁸

Tip
Delete a note
If you no longer need a note, you can delete it:

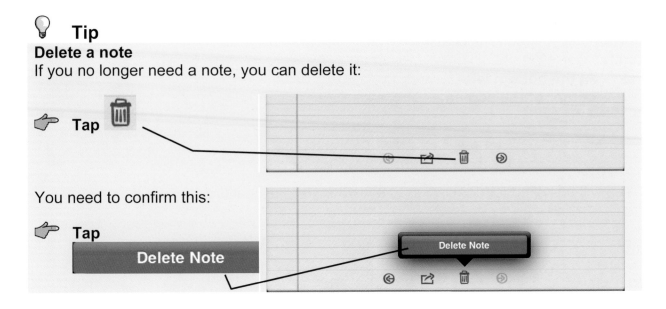

👉 **Tap** 🗑

You need to confirm this:

👉 **Tap**

Delete Note

4.6 Maps

With the *Maps* app you can search for a specific location and get directions for how to get there. To do this, you need to be connected to the Internet.

👉 **If necessary, turn on Wi-Fi** 👣^{10}

This is how you open the *Maps* app:

👉 **Tap** Maps

You will see the map of the country where you are located. Now you need to determine your current location:

👉 **At the bottom left corner of the screen, tap** ➤

You will be asked for permission to use your current location:

👉 **Tap** OK

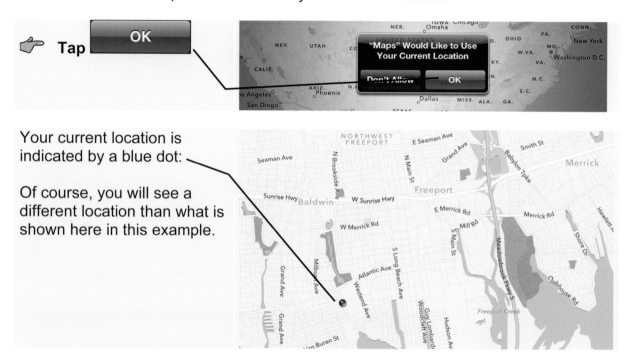

Your current location is indicated by a blue dot:

Of course, you will see a different location than what is shown here in this example.

This is how you can change the view of the map:

👉 **At the bottom right corner of the screen, tap the folded corner of the page** ➤

You can select a view:

Standard: regular view.

Satellite: satellite photo.

Hybrid: map and satellite photo combined.

 Tap **Hybrid**

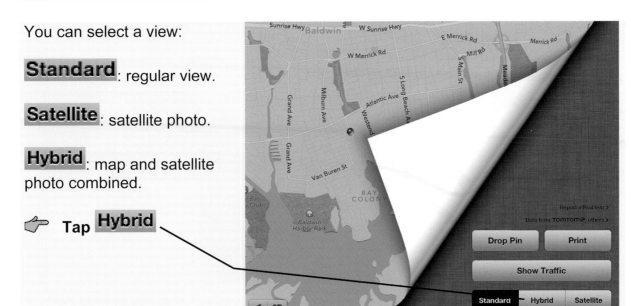

You will see a satellite photo with the names of the places in your current location:

Tip

Zooming in and out

Move two fingers apart from each other (spread), or move them towards each other (pinch) to zoom in or out.

4.7 Find a Location

You can use *Maps* to look for a specific location. You can search for a house or business address as well as a famous public place:

👉 **Tap the search box**

⌨️ **Type:** Guggenheim new york

👉 **Tap** Search

The location will be marked

with a red pin 📍 on the map:

Depending on the location you search for, you can see more pins:

You can use the black label to show more information about the location:

Tip

Detailed information

Many locations offer additional information if you tap the button, such as address information, the phone number and the website, if there is one:

To close the window:

☞ **Tap the map** ——

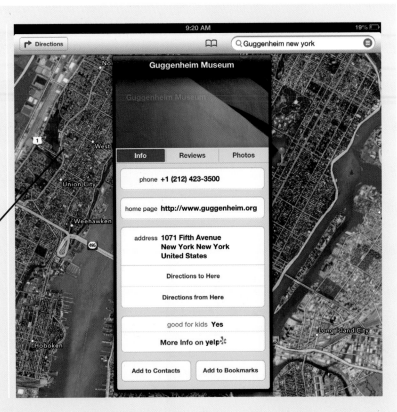

These are the functions of the buttons in this window:

Add to Contacts	Use this button to add the location you found to *Contacts*, as a contact.
Share Location	Use this button to open a new e-mail message containing information about this location.
Add to Bookmarks	Use this button to add a bookmark in *Maps*. This way, you can save the location and retrieve it later on, with the 📖 button.

4.8 Map out your Trip

Once you have found the desired location, you can plot a course for how to get there. This is how you do it:

👉 **Tap** [↱ **Directions**]

Here you will see the start and end point of the route:

With [⇅] you can switch the start and end point:

You can use the [🚌] and [🚶] buttons to view the route, the distance and the amount of time needed to walk to the destination or go by public transit:

To show the route by car:

👉 **Tap** [**Route**]

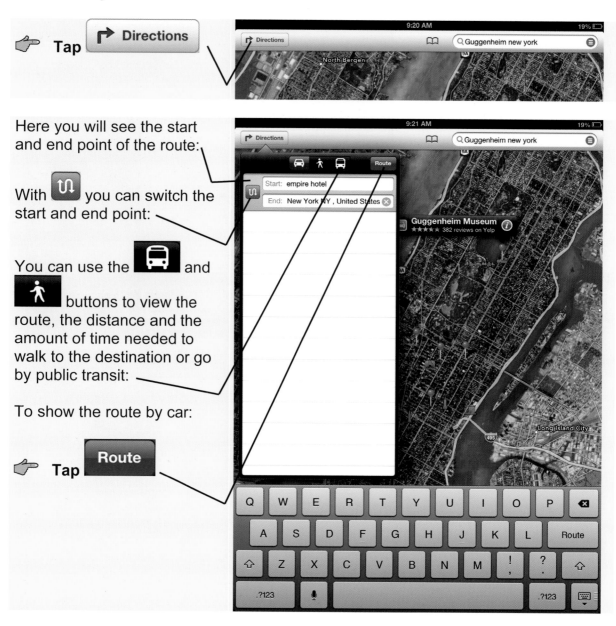

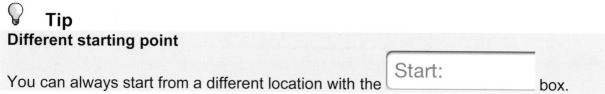

💡 **Tip**

Different starting point

You can always start from a different location with the [Start:] box.

You may see a safety warning:

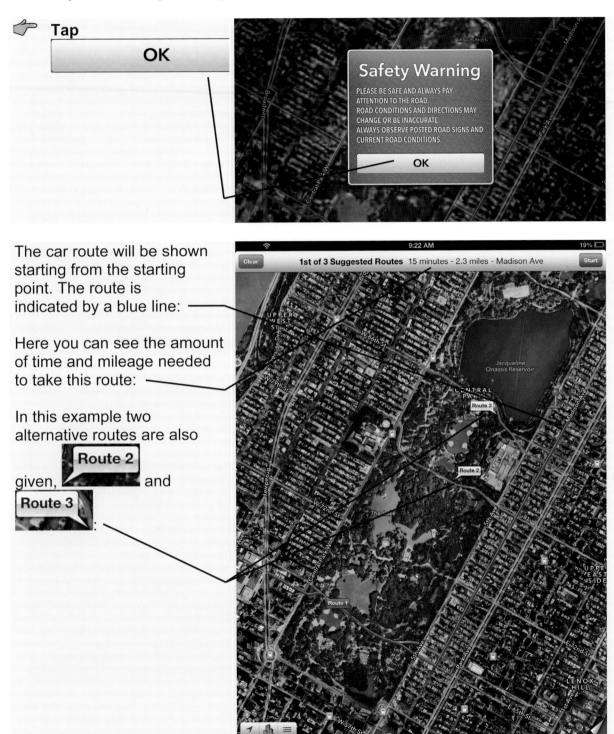

☞ **Tap**

| OK |

The car route will be shown starting from the starting point. The route is indicated by a blue line:

Here you can see the amount of time and mileage needed to take this route:

In this example two alternative routes are also given, **Route 2** and

Route 3 :

You can display a full set of directions for the route in an extra window:

👉 **Tap**

Unfortunately, you cannot (yet) print or e-mail the instructions.

Close the *Directions* window:

👉 **Tap**

But you can display the route step by step:

👉 **Tap** Start

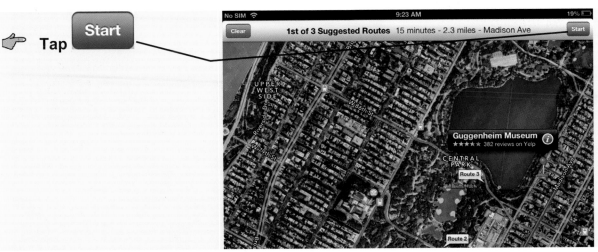

If you have chosen a route starting from your current location (as shown in this example), you can use your iPad as a navigation system. This is because the iPad has a built-in GPS feature. You will hear the spoken instructions and you will see

your current location on the screen:

As soon as you move, the

icon moves also and you will hear the next instruction. You can close the route:

👉 **Tap** End

If you have chosen a route from a specific location to another specific location (not you current location), then you will see the first step or leg of the route. Instructions are shown in a bright green block that looks like a highway sign:

To show the next step, simply tap the next green block:

To follow the entire route, tap the next green block continuously.

To close the screen, tap

End :

 Tap

You will again see your current location again.

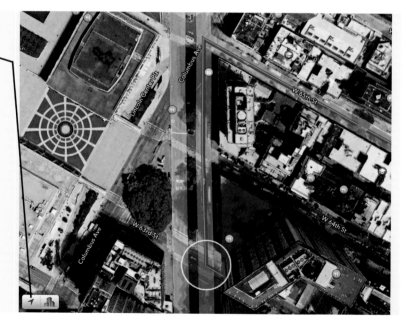

☞ **Go back to the home screen** 🦶8

☞ **If necessary, turn off Wi-Fi** 🦶7

💡 **Tip**
Display traffic information
You can display the traffic conditions on the main roads and highways on the map:

 ☞ **Tap** ,

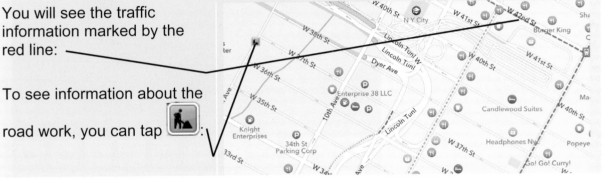

You will see the traffic
information marked by the
red line: ⎯

To see information about the

road work, you can tap :

4.9 Spotlight

Spotlight is your iPad's search utility. This is how you open *Spotlight*:

☞ **Swipe the home screen from left to right**

👉 **Tap** Notes

⌨️ **Type a note**

After you have finished typing:

👉 **Tap** Done

💡 **Tip**

Sound the Alarm

When the date and time of your reminder occurs, an alarm goes off and a small window pops up on your screen. If the iPad is in sleep mode:

👉 **Wake the iPad up from sleep** 👣²

You can view the reminder or close the window.

If you have stored a lot of reminders in this app, you can order them into lists. In this way, you can separate personal chores from work-related tasks, for instance. This is how you create a list:

👉 **Tap** Edit

👉 **Tap** Create New List...

⌨️ **Type a name for the list**

👉 **Tap** Done

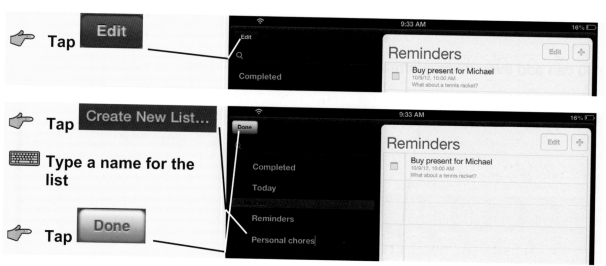

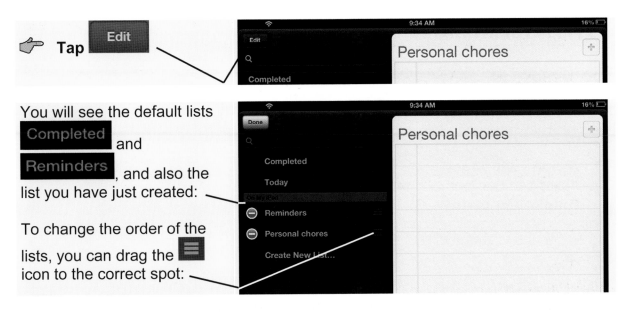

Tap **Edit**

You will see the default lists **Completed** and **Reminders**, and also the list you have just created:

To change the order of the lists, you can drag the ▤ icon to the correct spot:

If you no longer want to use a list, you can delete it:

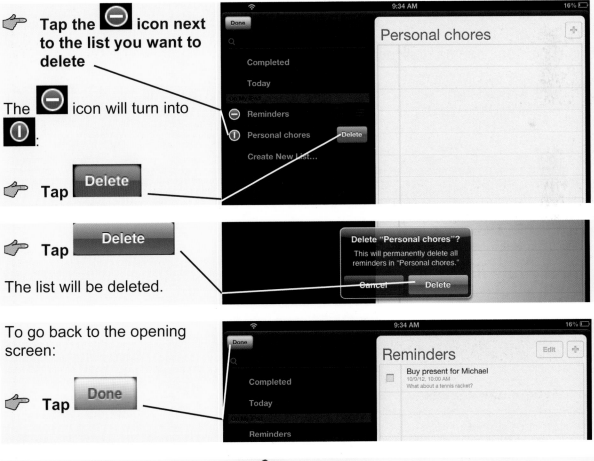

Tap the ⊖ icon next to the list you want to delete

The ⊖ icon will turn into ⊘ :

Tap **Delete**

Tap **Delete**

The list will be deleted.

To go back to the opening screen:

Tap **Done**

☞ **Go back to the home screen** 👣⁸

4.11 Notifications

The messages you receive on your iPad, such as new e-mail messages or other messages set to be displayed on your iPad, can all be viewed in the *Notification* center in a neatly arranged list. This way, you can quickly see which messages you have recently received. This is how you open the *Notifications*:

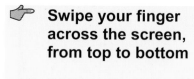 **Swipe your finger across the screen, from top to bottom**

The *Notification Center* will be opened:

In this example, you can see the reminder about Tennis lessons:

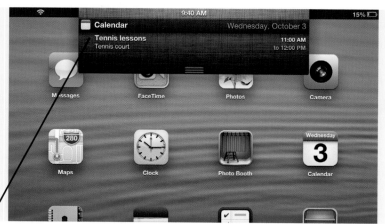

This is how you open a message:

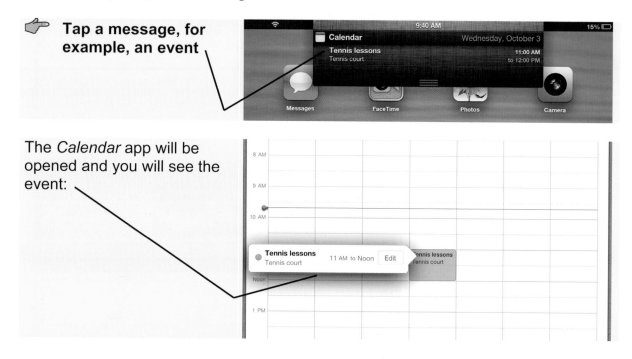 **Tap a message, for example, an event**

The *Calendar* app will be opened and you will see the event:

☞ **Go back to the home screen** 👣⁸

E-mail messages will not be displayed in the *Notification Center* by default; you need to change the settings in the *Settings* app:

☞ **Open the *Settings* app**

👉 **Tap** Notifications

👉 **Tap** Mail Badges

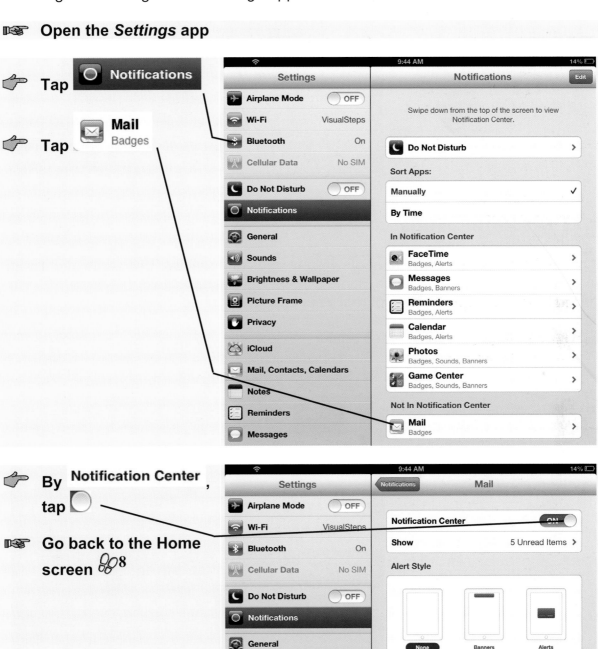

👉 **By** Notification Center **, tap** ◯

☞ **Go back to the Home screen** 👣⁸

☞ **Swipe your finger across the screen, from top to bottom**

In this example you will see a new e-mail message has been received:

4.12 Disabling Apps

By now, you have used a number of different apps on the iPad. Each time after using an app, you have returned to the Home screen. But the apps have not been disabled by this action. Actually, this is not really necessary, because the iPad uses very little power in sleep mode, and you have the advantage of being able to continue at the same spot, once you start working again.

Nevertheless, it is possible to close the apps, if you want. This is how you do it:

☞ **Press the Home button twice**

☞ **Put your finger on one of the apps**

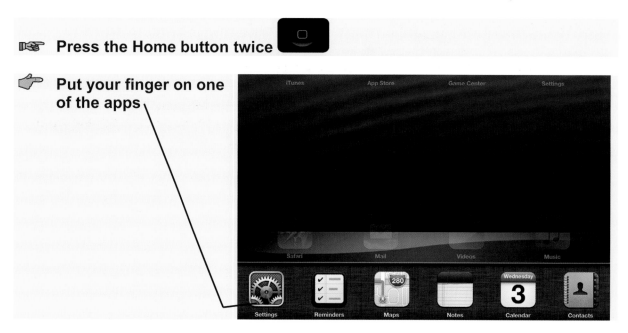

Now the apps will start jiggling, you will see a red icon 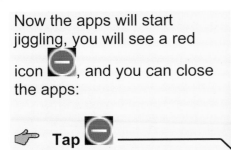, and you can close the apps:

👉 **Tap**

The app will be closed.

You can close the other apps in the same way:

👉 **Tap the** **icon for the other apps too**

👉 **Press the home button** ⬜

👉 **If you want, put the iPad into sleep mode or turn it off** 👣¹

In this chapter you have learned more about some of the standard apps that are installed on your iPad. The following exercises will let you practice using these apps.

4.13 Exercises

🐾

To be able to quickly apply the things you have learned, you can work through these exercises. Have you forgotten how to do something? Use the numbers next to the footsteps 🐾^{1} to look up the item in the appendix *How Do I Do That Again?*

Exercise 1: Contacts

In this exercise you will practice adding and editing contacts.

☞   If necessary, wake the iPad up from sleep or turn it on. 🐾^{2}

☞   Open the *Contacts* app. 🐾^{46}

☞   Add a new contact. 🐾^{45}

☞   Open the information about the contact to change it. 🐾^{47}

☞   Change the *mobile* label to *home*. 🐾^{48}

☞   Save the changes. 🐾^{49}

☞   Go back to the home screen. 🐾^{8}

Exercise 2: Calendar

In this exercise you will practice adding a new event to the *Calendar* app.

☞   Open the *Calendar* app. 🐾^{50}

☞   Select the *Day* view. 🐾^{51}

☞   Go to Today. 🐾^{52}

☞   Skip to the day after tomorrow. 🐾^{53}

☞   Open a new event. 🐾^{54}

☞   Enter these items: 🐾^{55}
     name: lunch, location: Lunchroom The Jolly Joker.

☞ Change the times: starts: `12:00 PM`, ends `1:00 PM`. 🐾**56**

☞ Save the changes 🐾**49** and return to the home screen. 🐾**8**

Exercise 3: Maps

In this exercise you are going to look for a location.

☞ If necessary, turn on Wi-Fi. 🐾**10**

☞ Open the *Maps* app. 🐾**57**

☞ Find your current location. 🐾**58**

☞ Change the view to *Satellite*. 🐾**59**

☞ Search for this location: `Arc de Triomphe Paris`. 🐾**60**

☞ Get more information on the location. 🐾**61**

☞ Map out a trip from Rue de Rivoli to the Arc de Triomphe. 🐾**62**

☞ Display a full set of directions for the route. 🐾**63**

☞ Go back to the home screen. 🐾**8**

☞ If necessary, turn off Wi-Fi. 🐾**7**

Exercise 4: Spotlight

In this exercise you are going to practice searching with *Spotlight*.

☞ Open *Spotlight*. 🐾**64**

☞ Search for one of your contacts. 🐾**65**

☞ Tap the desired search result.

☞ Go back to the home screen. 🐾**8**

☞ If you want, put the iPad into sleep mode or turn it off. 🐾**1**

4.14 Background Information

Dictionary

Calendar	An app that lets you keep track of your appointments and activities.
Camera Roll	The name of the folder that contains the photos you have made with your iPad, or stored with your iPad, for example, a picture from an e-mail attachment or a website.
Contacts	An app that you can use to manage your contacts.
Event	An appointment in the *Calendar* app.
Field	Part of the information you can enter about a contact. For example, *First name* and *Postal code* are fields.
Google Calendar	A *Google* service that lets you keep a calendar or agenda.
Google Contacts	A *Google* service that allows you to store and manage contacts.
Label	The name of a field.
Maps	An app where you can look for locations and addresses, view satellite photos and plan routes.
Notes	An app with which you can take notes.
Outlook	An e-mail program that is part of the *Microsoft Office* suite.
Spotlight	The search utility on the iPad.
Synchronize	Literally: make even. Not only can you synchronize your iPad with the content of your *iTunes Library*, but also the information about your contacts or calendar events.
Windows Contacts	*Windows* service that lets you store and manage contacts.
Yahoo! Address Book	*Yahoo!* Service that lets you store and manage contacts.

Source: User Guide iPad, Wikipedia

4.15 Tips

  Tip

Add a photo
If you have a nice picture of your contact stored on your iPad, you can add this photo to his or her contact information. In *Chapter 6 Photos* you can read how to take a picture with the iPad, and how to transfer photos to your iPad. This is to add an existing photo to your contact:

☞ **Tap the desired contact**

☞ **Tap** Edit

☞ **Tap** add photo

☞ **Tap** **Choose Photo**

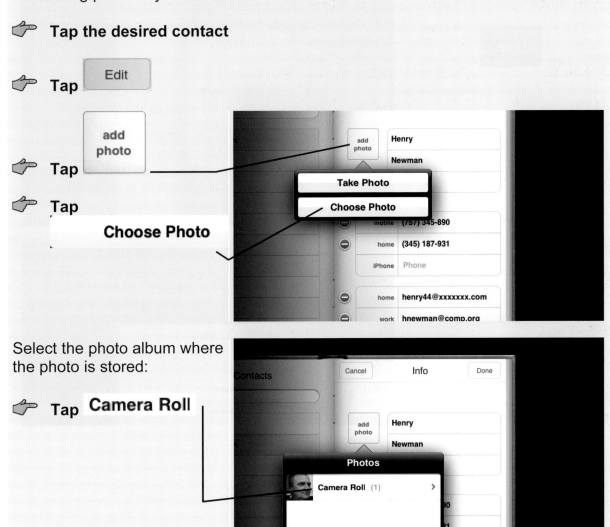

Select the photo album where the photo is stored:

☞ **Tap** **Camera Roll**

- Continue on the next page -

Tip

Add an event from an e-mail message

Mail recognizes dates in e-mail messages and can insert them into your calendar. After a date has been recognized, you can quickly add an event to your calendar:

☞ **Tap the date**

November 10th

☞ **Tap**

Create Event

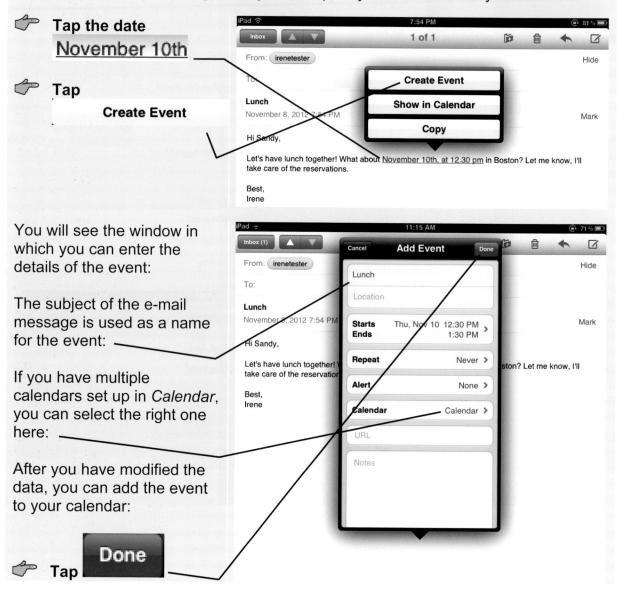

You will see the window in which you can enter the details of the event:

The subject of the e-mail message is used as a name for the event:

If you have multiple calendars set up in *Calendar*, you can select the right one here:

After you have modified the data, you can add the event to your calendar:

☞ **Tap** Done

Tip

Look up a contact on the map

A useful function in the *Maps* app is being able to search for your contacts on a map:

☞ **Tap** 📖

☞ **Tap the desired contact**

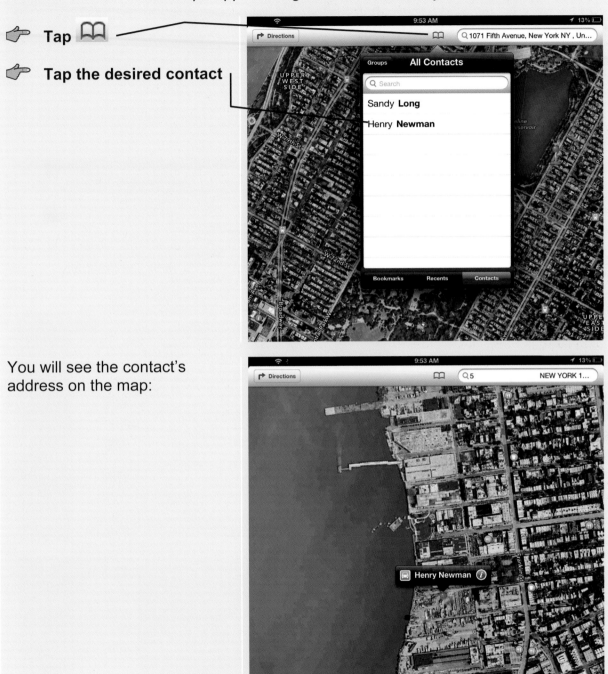

You will see the contact's address on the map:

💡 Tip

Display Google Calendar

Do you use *Google Calendar* to keep track of appointments and activities? And have you set up your *Gmail* account on the iPad? Then you can set your *Gmail* account to display your calendar on the iPad too.

☞ **Open the *Settings* app** ⁶

👉 **Tap** ✉️ **Mail, Contacts, Calendars**

Open your *Gmail* account settings:

👉 **Tap Gmail**

👉 **By 📅 Calendars, tap the ⬭ OFF button**

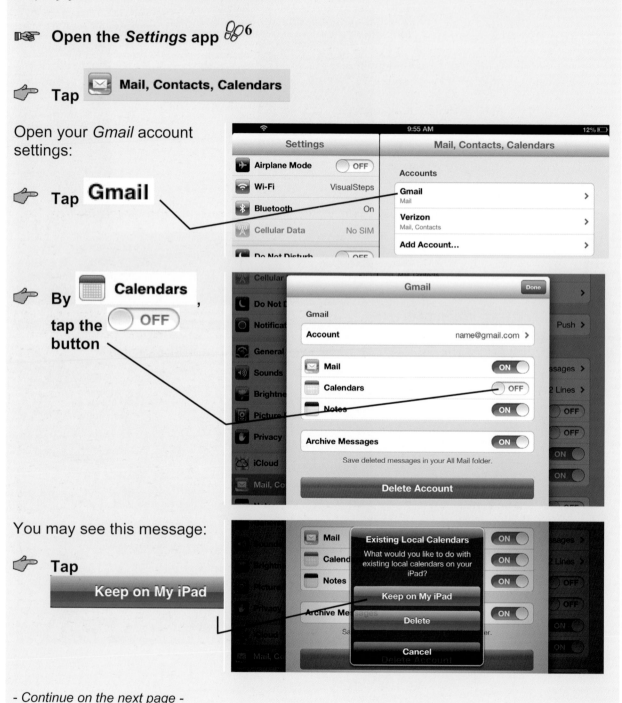

You may see this message:

👉 **Tap** **Keep on My iPad**

- Continue on the next page -

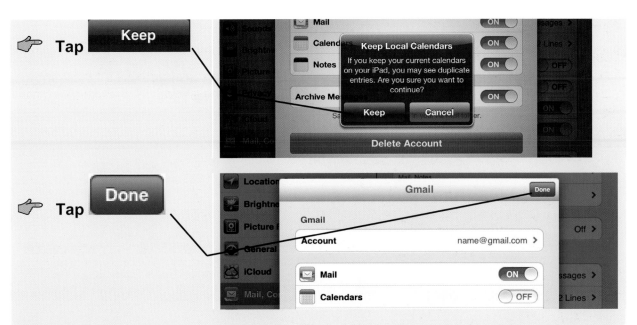

Tap

Now the events from your *Google Calendar* will be displayed in the *Calendar* app on your iPad.

💡 Tip

Synchronize contacts

Do you manage your contacts already on your computer? Then you might be able to synchronize these contacts with your iPad. You can synchronize with contacts from *Outlook*, *Windows Contacts*, *Google Contacts*, and *Yahoo! Address Book*.

☞ Connect your iPad to the computer

The *iTunes* program will automatically open:

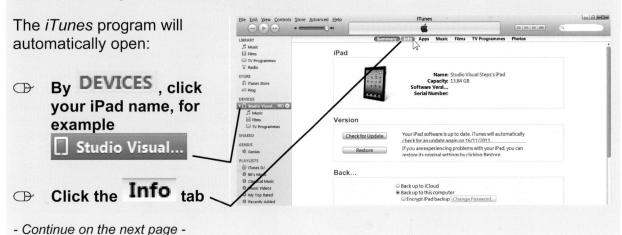

⊕ By **DEVICES**, click your iPad name, for example **☐ Studio Visual...**

⊕ Click the **Info** tab

- Continue on the next page -

In this example, the contacts will be synchronized with *Windows Contacts*:

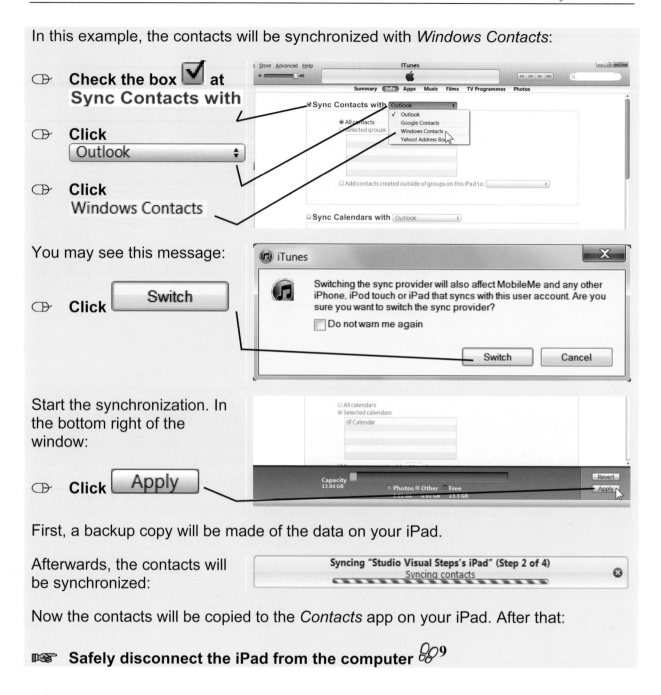

- ☞ **Check the box ☑ at Sync Contacts with**

- ☞ **Click**
  Outlook

- ☞ **Click**
  Windows Contacts

You may see this message:

- ☞ **Click Switch**

Start the synchronization. In the bottom right of the window:

- ☞ **Click Apply**

First, a backup copy will be made of the data on your iPad.

Afterwards, the contacts will be synchronized:

Now the contacts will be copied to the *Contacts* app on your iPad. After that:

☞ **Safely disconnect the iPad from the computer** 🦶🦶**9**

Tip

Synchronize with Google Contacts

If you want to synchronize with contacts from *Google Contacts*, first, you might need to give *iTunes* permission to access your data in *Google Contacts*:

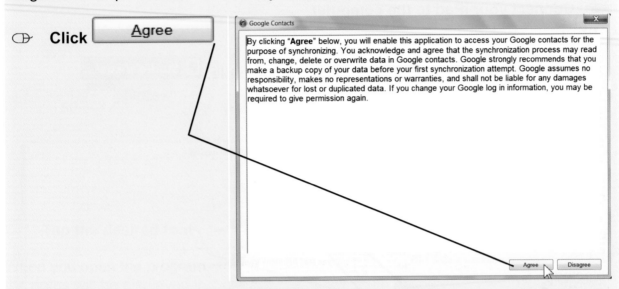

☞ **Click** ⎡ Agree ⎤

Next, you will need to enter your *Google ID* (e-mail address) and your password:

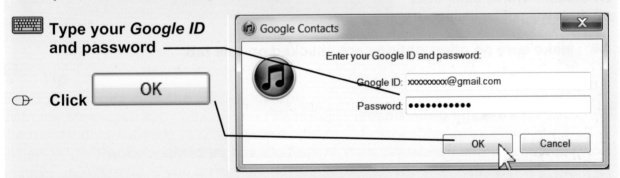

⌨ **Type your *Google ID* and password**

☞ **Click** ⎡ OK ⎤

In the bottom right of the window:

☞ **Click** ⎡ Apply ⎤

Now you will be asked whether you want to merge or replace the contact data:

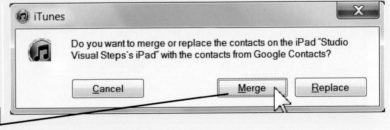

☞ **Click** ⎡ Merge ⎤

The contacts will be synchronized.

5.1 Creating an Apple ID

If you want to download apps in the *App Store*, you will need to have an *iTunes App Store Account*. This is also called an *Apple ID*.

 Please note:

In this example, an *iTunes App Store Account* will be created without linking a credit card to this account. By using an *iTunes Gift Card* you will be able to purchase apps in the *App Store*. In the next section you can read all about the *iTunes Gift Card*.

Open the *App Store*:

☞ **Wake the iPad up from sleep or turn it on** $\mathcal{QP}2$

☞ **If necessary, turn on Wi-Fi** $\mathcal{QP}10$

☞ **Tap** App Store

Now the *App Store* will be opened.

You will see the  page, where a number of new apps are on display.

To create an *iTunes App Store Account* without selecting a payment method, you need to download at least one free app. Use the search box to look for a popular free app:

👉 **Tap the search box**

⌨ **Type:** `weather`

Right away, you will see a number of suggestions:

👉 **Tap**
   the weather channel®

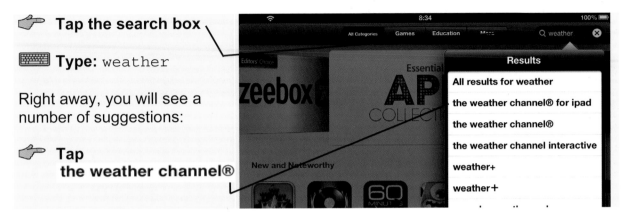

Here is how to download this app:

👉 **By**
   the weather channel®

   tap FREE

The FREE button will turn into INSTALL APP :

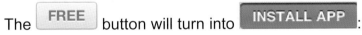

👉 **Tap** INSTALL APP

Before you can install the app, you need to sign in with your *Apple ID*:

☞ **Tap**

United States has already been entered: ——

☞ **Tap** **Next**

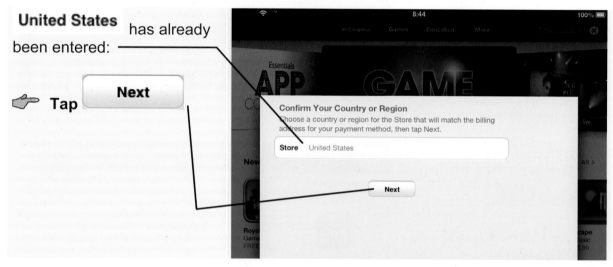

You will see the terms and conditions:

To view the rest of the text:

☞ **Swipe the New Account screen upwards**

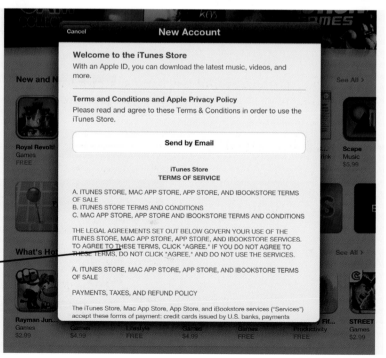

When you reach the bottom
of the text:

👉 **Tap** Agree

Confirm once again that you agree to the conditions:

👉 **Tap** Agree

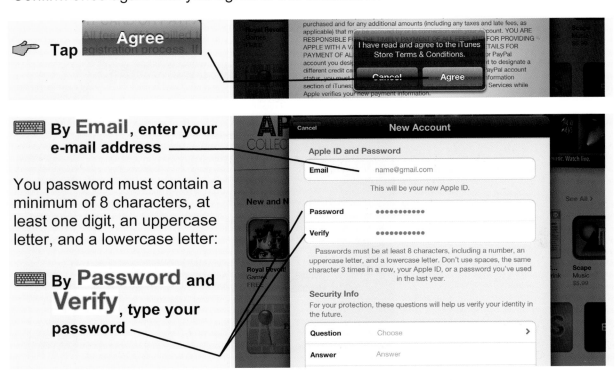

⌨ By **Email**, **enter your
e-mail address**

You password must contain a
minimum of 8 characters, at
least one digit, an uppercase
letter, and a lowercase letter:

⌨ By **Password** and
Verify, **type your
password**

Next, select questions that will act as a hint to help you remember your password.
You can use these security questions to retrieve your password, if you forget it:

👉 **Tap Question**

👉 **Tap a question**

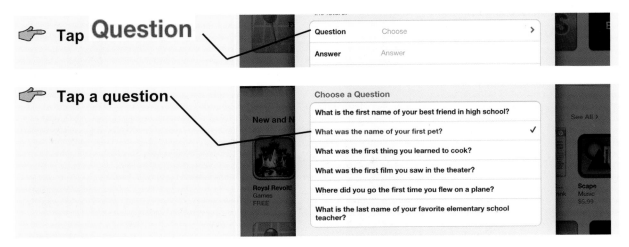

⌨️ By **Answer**, type the answer to this question ———

☞ **Do the same with the other questions and answers**

Now, enter your date of birth:

👉 Tap **Month** ———

👉 **Tap your birth month**

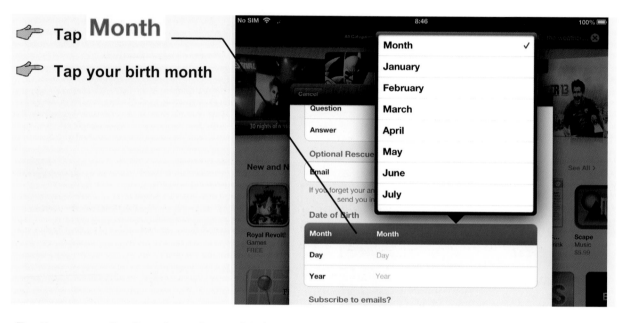

Do the same for the day of your birth:

👉 Tap **Day** ———

👉 **If necessary, swipe upwards across the list**

👉 **Tap the day of your birth**

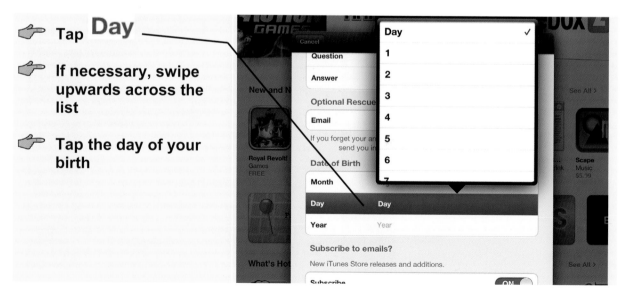

☞ **Tap** **Year**

⌨ **Type the year of your birth**

You do not need to subscribe to the *iTunes* and *Apple* e-mail services. To turn it off:

☞ **By**
Subscribe to email
tap **ON**

☞ **Drag upwards across the screen**

☞ **Tap** **Next**

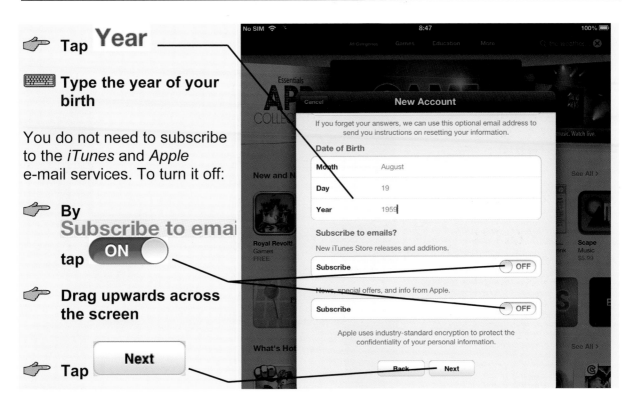

Now the *Billing Information* window will be opened. If you want, you can link a *Visa*, *MasterCard* or *American Express* credit card to your *Apple ID*. In this example we will create an *Apple ID* without selecting a payment method:

☞ **Tap** **None**

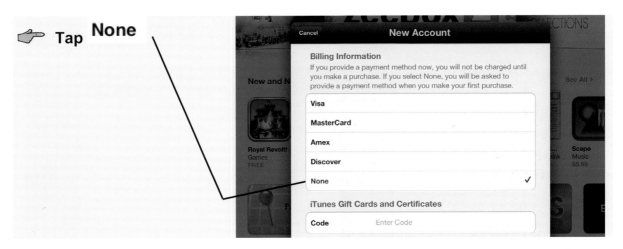

HELP! I see a slightly different window.

If you see this window you will need to do the following:

Tap **Visa**

Tap **None**

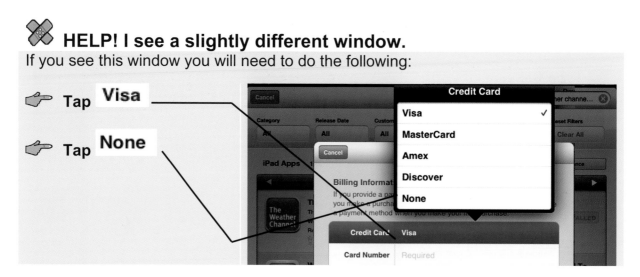

Now you need to enter your name, address and phone number:

Swipe upwards over the screen

Tap **Title**

Tap the appropriate title

Type the required data

Tap **Next**

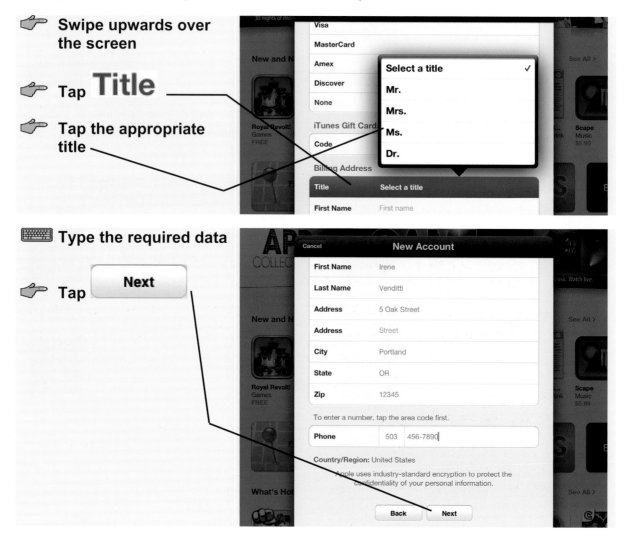

The *Verify Your Account* window will be opened:

To verify your *Apple ID,* a
confirmation e-mail containing
a hyperlink has been sent to
the e-mail you submitted:

☞ **Go back to the home screen** 𝓑𝓑⁸

☞ **Open the *Mail* app** 𝓑𝓑¹¹

☞ **Open the message from *Apple*** 𝓑𝓑²³

☞ **Tap** Verify Now >

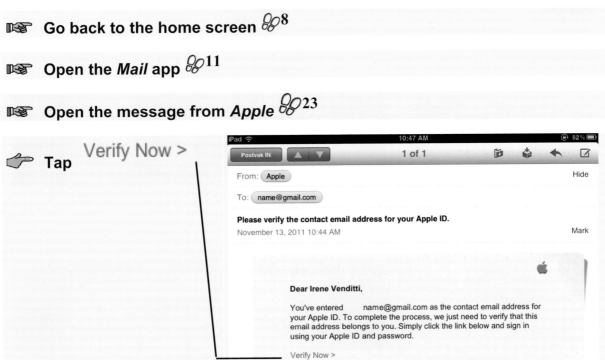

A web page will be opened. Here you need to sign in with your *Apple ID* and your
password, in order to verify your e-mail address:

⌨ **In the first box, type
your e-mail address**

This is your Apple ID

⌨ **In the second box,
type your password**

☞ **Tap**

Verify Address

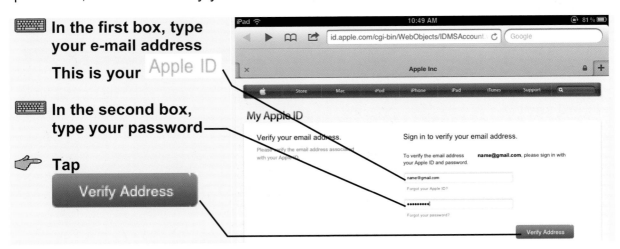

Tap

Now you will return to the *App Store*. Here you will need to sign in once again, with your *Apple ID* and password:

Tap

HELP! I see a different window.
If you see this window:

Tap

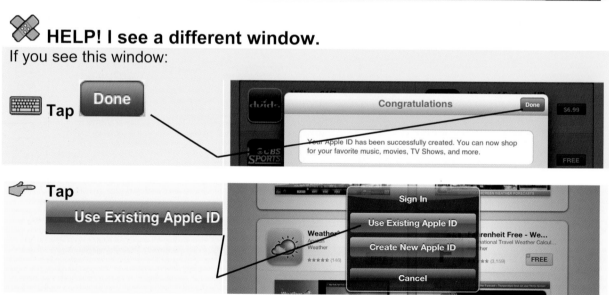

Tap

You need to sign in with your *Apple ID* in order to install the app. You will do this in the next section.

5.2 Downloading and Installing a Free App

Now you can sign in with your *Apple ID* so you can download the *Weather Channel Interactive* app:

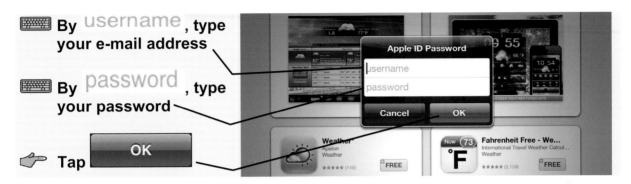

⌨ **By** username **, type your e-mail address**

⌨ **By** password **, type your password**

☞ **Tap** OK

You will see that the app is immediately downloaded and installed:

The app is installed when you see the button OPEN :

You do not need to open the app right now.

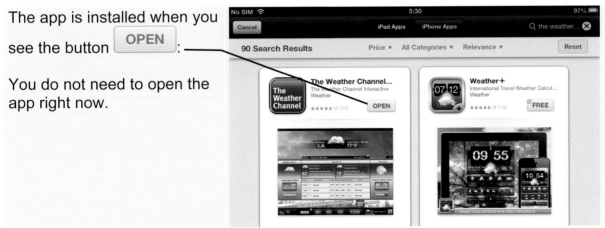

☞ **Go back to the home screen** 👣**8**

You will see the app at the
second page:

 Tip
Manage your apps
By default, the new app will be put on a blank page. In *section 5.6 Managing Apps*
you can read how to move your apps around and how to place them on other pages.

In the following section you will learn how to use an *iTunes Gift Card* to purchase an
app.

5.3 The iTunes Gift Card

The *iTunes Gift Card* is a prepaid card that you can use to purchase items in the *App
Store.* By using an *iTunes Gift Card*, you can avoid using a credit card.

 Tip
iTunes Gift Card
The *iTunes Gift Card* comes in denominations of $15, $25 and $50. You can
purchase these cards from the *Apple Online Store*, at your *Apple* retailer and at
thousands of other retailers across the USA, the UK and Australia.

You can also get the *iTunes Gift Card* at www.instantitunescodes.com.
This web store allows you to pay
online and you will receive the code for
the card by e-mail, right away. *iTunes
Gift Cards* purchased at this store are
only valid in the United States.

 Please note:
To be able to follow the examples in the next section, you need to have an *iTunes
Gift Card* available. If you do not (yet) have such a card, you can just read the text.

☞ **Open the *App Store*** 🐾85

At the bottom of the page, you will find the link to redeem an *iTunes Gift Card*:

Now you will see a window where you can enter the code for your *iTunes Gift Card*.

You will find the code under the scratch layer on the back of the card: ——————

☞ **Carefully remove the scratch layer**

Now you will see a code composed of 16 digits and letters that you need to enter:

⌨ **Type the code**

Although the code on the *iTunes Gift Card* contains capital letters, you can just type lower-case letters.

☞ **Tap** Redeem

Before you can redeem the code, you might need to sign in with your *Apple ID*:

☞ **Tap** Continue

Your *Apple ID* has already been entered:

⌨ **Type your password**

☞ **Tap** OK

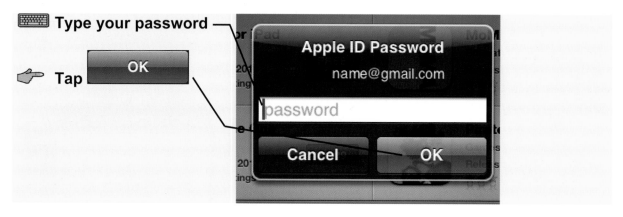

You will see a confirmation:

In this example, the *Apple ID* has a credit of $10:

5.4 Buying and Installing an App

Now that you have purchased a prepaid credit for your *Apple ID*, you will be able to buy apps in the *App Store*. Previously, you used the search box to look for an app. But you can also view the Top Charts that display today's most popular apps:

☞ **Tap** Charts

Now the *Thank you* window will disappear:

☞ **Tap** Charts

You will see the Top 9 paid and free iPad apps:

On your iPad, these lists will look different, because they change very frequently.

This is how you can view the rest of the chart:

👉 **Swipe upwards over one of the lists**

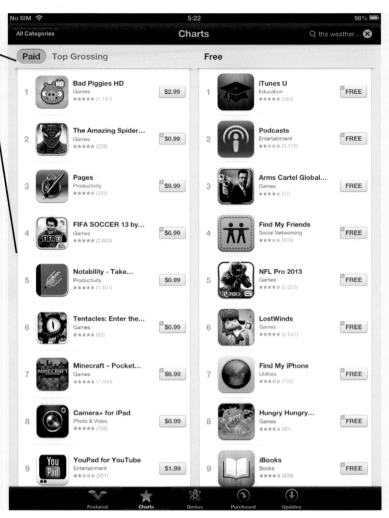

Now you will see the numbers 6-14.

Please note:

In the example below we will be purchasing an app. You can decide whether you want to follow the steps and buy an app. Of course, you do not need to buy exactly the same app as in this example.

 Please note:

You will only be able to follow the steps below if you have redeemed an *iTunes Gift Card* or if you have linked your credit card to your *Apple ID*. If you have not (yet) done this, you can just read through the rest of this section.

In this example we will purchase the *Weather+* app. First we will search for this app:

You can still see the text 'the weather channel' in the search box:

☞ **Tap the search box**

The window with the suggestions will be opened:

☞ **Swipe upwards across the screen**

☞ **Tap**

You will see additional
information about this app:

If you want to buy the app:

☞ **Tap**

The button will turn

into **BUY APP**.

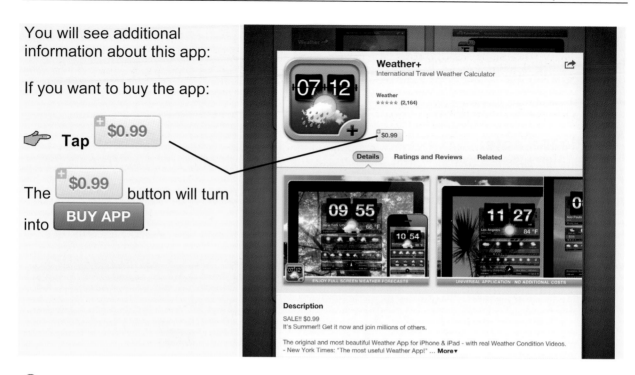

💡 Tip

iPhone and iPad

The plus sign 🔲 on the ⬚$0.99 button indicates that the app is suitable for the
iPhone, as well as for the iPad. In the *Tips* at the end of this chapter you can read
how to transfer the items you have purchased to *iTunes* on the computer and how to
synchronize the apps on your iPhone or iPad with *iTunes*.

☞ **Tap** **BUY APP**

Before you can buy the app, you may have to sign in again with your *Apple ID*. This is a security measure, to prevent someone else from using your *iTunes* credit or credit card to buy things, for instance if you lend your iPad to someone else.

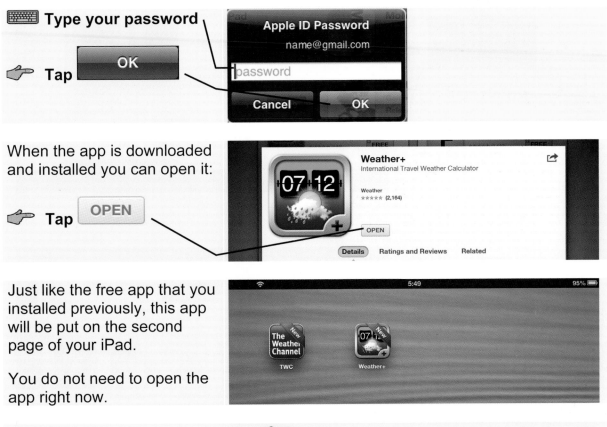

Type your password

☞ **Tap** OK

When the app is downloaded and installed you can open it:

☞ **Tap** OPEN

Just like the free app that you installed previously, this app will be put on the second page of your iPad.

You do not need to open the app right now.

☞ **Go back to the home screen** 8

5.5 Sign Out From the App Store

After you have signed in with your *Apple ID*, you will stay logged on for 15 minutes. During that period you can purchase items without having to enter your password again.

❧ Please note:

In some game apps, such as the popular game *Smurfs Village*, you can buy fake money or credits during the game and use it for bargaining. These *smurfberries* are paid with the money from your remaining *iTunes* credit or from your credit card. If you let your (grand) children play such a game, they can purchase items in these first 15 minutes without having to enter your password. So, it is better to sign out first.

☞ Open the *App Store* ᕴ⁸⁵

You will see the page with the suggestions:

☞ **Tap**

Go to the bottom of the page:

☞ **Swipe upwards across the screen**

Here you can see how much credit you still have left on your *Apple ID* account: ——

To sign out:

☞ **Tap**

Apple ID: name@gm...

☞ **Tap**

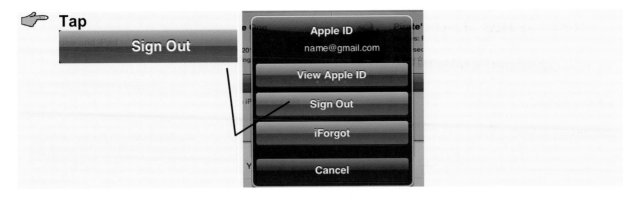

You will see the *Featured* page again:

Here you can see that you
are signed off:

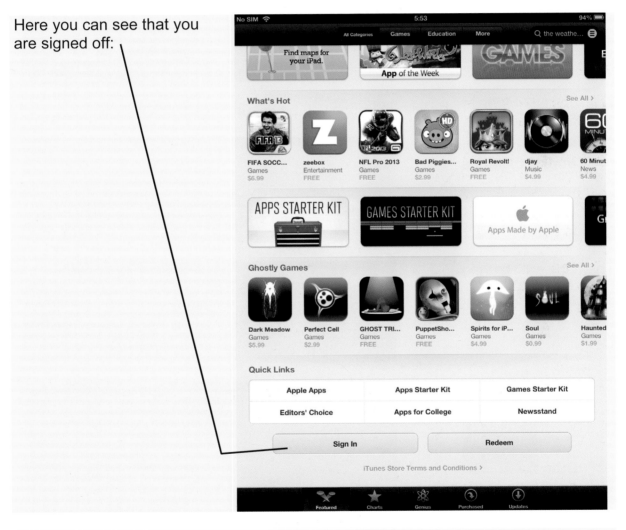

☞ **Go back to the home screen** ✂8

5.6 Managing Apps

You can completely adjust the order of the apps on your iPad to your own taste, by moving the apps around. This is how you scroll to the second page with the apps you just bought:

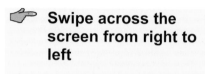 **Swipe across the screen from right to left**

Now you will see the page with the apps you have purchased:

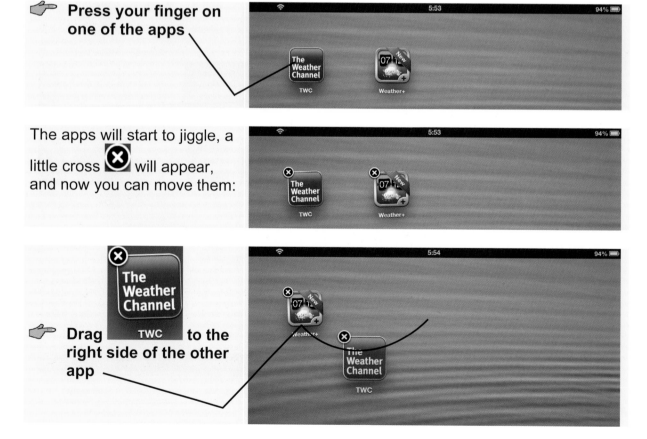

☞ **Press your finger on one of the apps**

The apps will start to jiggle, a little cross ⊗ will appear, and now you can move them:

☞ **Drag** *The Weather Channel TWC* **to the right side of the other app**

Now the apps have changed place.

You can also move an app to a different page. This is how you move an app to the home screen:

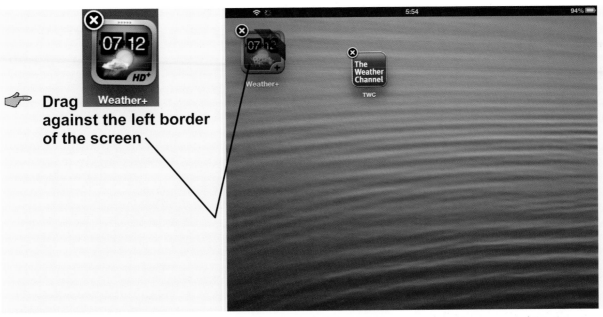

Drag against the left border of the screen

When you see the home screen:

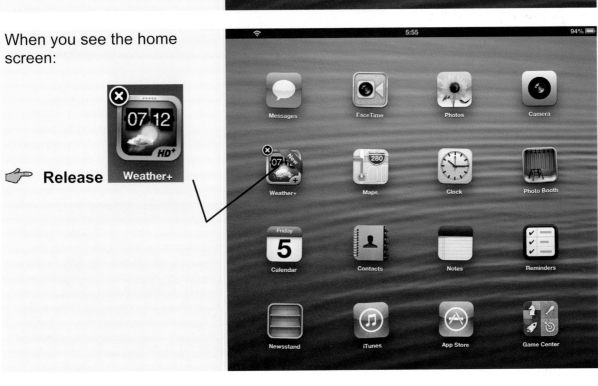

Release

Now the app has been placed between the other apps on the home screen:

Of course, you can also change the order of the apps on this page. For now, this will not be necessary.

☞ **Flip to the second page** ⌭⌭^86

☞ **Move the app you just bought to the home screen** ⌭⌭^87

You can also store related apps in a separate folder. Here is how to do that:

☞ **Drag** ... **on top of** ...

A suitable name will be
suggested for the new folder:

If you want you can also
change this name:

 **Tap the name**

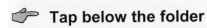 **Type the desired name**

If you are satisfied with the
name:

 **Tap below the folder**

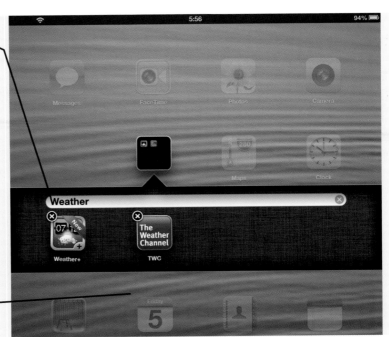

Now you will see this folder
on the home screen:

This is how to stop the apps from jiggling:

 **Press the Home button**

Now the apps have stopped moving. To view the contents of the folder:

 👉 **Tap** Weather

You will see both the apps in this folder:

You can store up to a maximum of twenty apps in the same folder.

This is how you remove the app from the folder again:

☞ **Make the apps jiggle** 🐾**88**

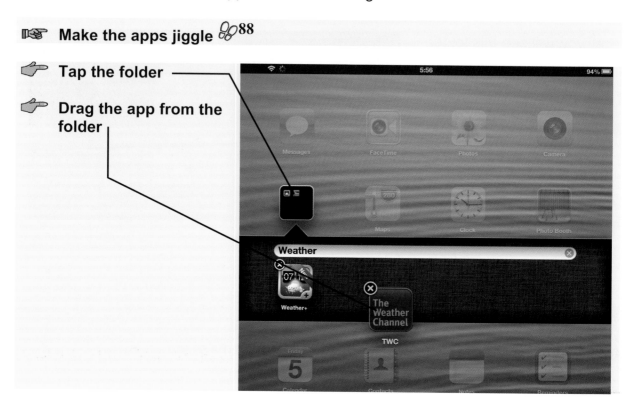

👉 **Tap the folder**

👉 **Drag the app from the folder**

Now the app has returned to the home screen:

If you remove the other app from the folder too, the folder will disappear.

☞ **Drag the other app from the folder** 𝒪𝒪**98**

Stop the apps from jiggling again:

☞ **Press the Home button**

5.7 Deleting an App

Have you downloaded an app that turns out to be a bit disappointing? You can easily delete such an app.

☞ **Make the apps jiggle** 𝒪𝒪**88**

With the digital zoom you can zoom in on an object, up to five times. You can only do this by using the camera on the back of the iPad. This is how you zoom in:

☞ **Move your thumb and index finger apart, on the screen**

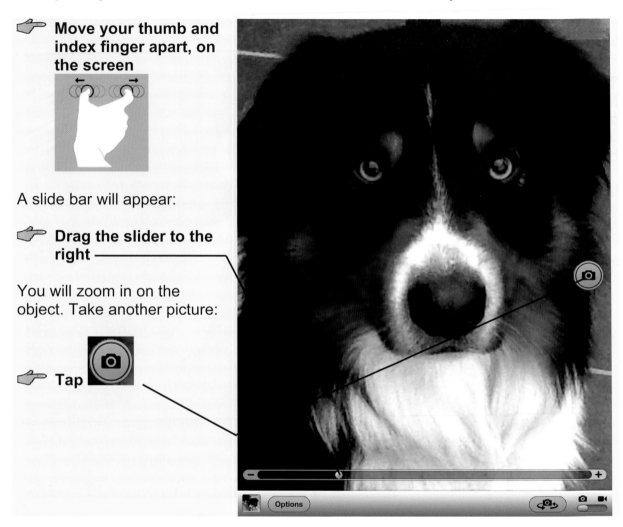

A slide bar will appear:

☞ **Drag the slider to the right**

You will zoom in on the object. Take another picture:

☞ **Tap**

This is how you zoom out again:

☞ **Drag the slider to the left**

Or:

☞ **Move your thumb and index finger towards each other, on the screen**

Tip

Self-portrait

You can also use the camera at the front of the iPad. For instance, for taking a picture of yourself. This is how you switch to the front camera:

 **Tap**

Now you will see the image recorded by the front camera:

You can take a picture in the same way as you previously did with the back camera. Only, the front camera does not have a digital zoom option.

This is how you switch to the back camera again:

  Tap

♀ Tip

Use the grid

Do you want to position something exactly in the middle of a picture? Then you can use the grid to help you. You can turn the grid option on like this:

☞ Tap **Options**

☞ By **Grid** tap ◯ OFF

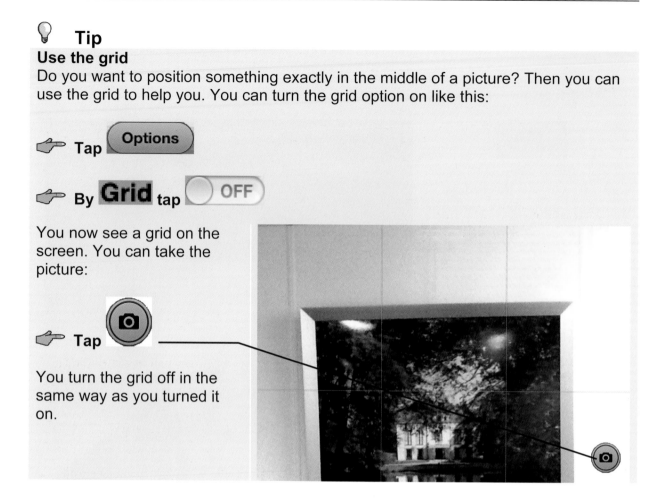

You now see a grid on the screen. You can take the picture:

☞ Tap 📷

You turn the grid off in the same way as you turned it on.

6.2 Shooting Videos

You can also use the back camera of the iPad for shooting videos:

 If necessary, turn your iPad a quarter turn, so it is in the horizontal position

♀ Tip

Turn sideways

Do you intend to play your video on a TV or on a larger screen? Then position your iPad sideways, in landscape mode. This way, your image will fill the entire screen.

👉 **Drag the slider** ⬜ **to**
   🎥

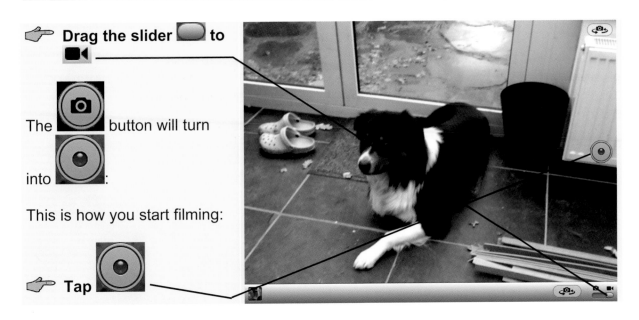

The 📷 button will turn

into 🔘 :

This is how you start filming:

👉 **Tap** 🔘

While you are shooting the film, the red light on the 🔘 button will keep blinking.

This is how you stop filming:

👉 **Tap** 🔘

You can reset the *Camera* app for taking pictures:

👉 **Drag the slider** ⬜ **to** 📷

☞ **Go back to the home screen** 🦶[8]

☞ **If you want, turn the iPad a quarter turn until it is in upright position again**

In the *Tips* at the end of this chapter you can read how to play a video on your iPad.

6.3 Photo Booth

The *Photo Booth* app allows you to add eight different types of effects to your photo right as you are taking the picture. You can use both cameras on the iPad with this app. This is how you open the *Photo Booth* app:

☞ **Tap** Photo Booth

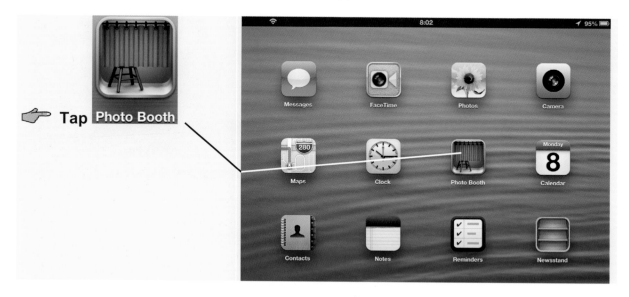

You will see yourself in the image that is recorded by the front camera:

☞ **Tap an effect, for example** Kaleidoscope

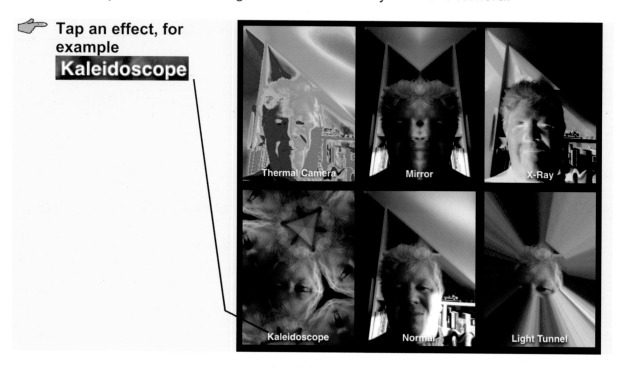

You will see a larger image of this effect. Now you can take a picture:

☞ **Tap**

💡 Tip
Additional options

With the ⟲🄾⟳ button you can switch to the back camera: ———

With the 🌀 button you can display the opening screen of the *Photo Booth* app, where you can select a different effect: ——

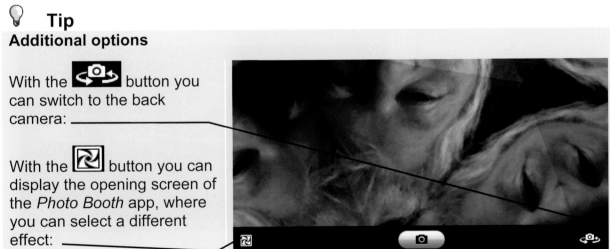

☞ **Go back to the home screen** 👣**8**

6.4 Viewing Photos

You have taken a number of pictures with your iPad. You can view these photos with the *Photos* app. This is how you open the app:

In the bottom of the screen:

☞ **Tap** **Photos**

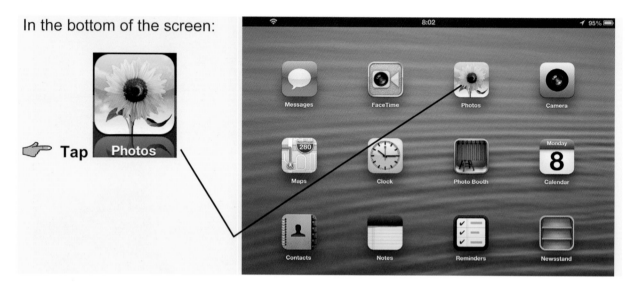

💡 **Tip**

Transfer photos to the iPad with iTunes
You can also use *iTunes* to transfer photos taken with your digital camera to your iPad. Very handy, if you want to show your favorite pictures to others. In the *Tips* at the end of this chapter you can read how to do this.

You will see the thumbprints of the pictures you have taken:

In this example you can also see a video, in between the photos: ——

☞ **Tap the fourth photo**

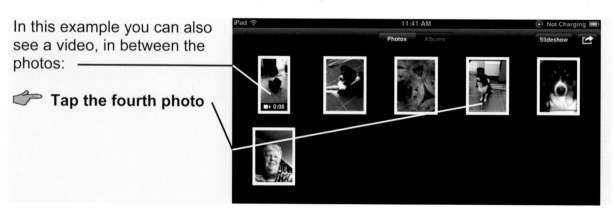

The photo will be displayed on a full screen. This is how you scroll to the next photo:

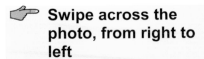 **Swipe across the photo, from right to left**

You will see the next photo. You can go back to the previous photo:

 Swipe across the photo, from left to right

💡 **Tip**

Delete a photo
You can easily delete a photo you have taken with the iPad from your iPad:

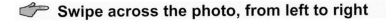 **If necessary, tap the photo**

 In the top right of your screen, tap

👉 **Tap** ▭ **Delete Photo**

You can also zoom in on a photo. For this, you use the same touch actions (pinching movements) you used earlier on, while surfing the Internet:

 Move your thumb and index finger apart, on the screen

You will zoom in on the photo:

💡 **Tip**

Move away
You can move the photo you have just zoomed in on, by dragging your finger across the screen.

This is how you zoom out again:

 Move your thumb and index finger towards each other, on the screen

You will again see the regular view of the photo.
You can view a slideshow of all the pictures on your iPad. Here is how to do that:

☞ **If necessary, tap the photo** ──

☞ **Tap** **Slideshow**

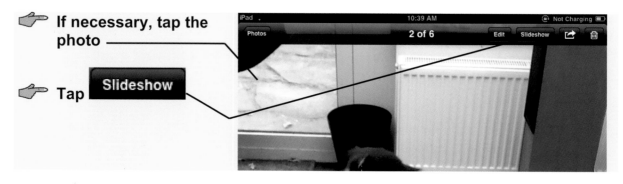

Before the slideshow starts, you can set various options:

Here you can set the type of transition between the photos:

If you have stored music on your iPad, you can play music during the slideshow:

This is how you start the slideshow:

☞ **Tap**

Start Slideshow

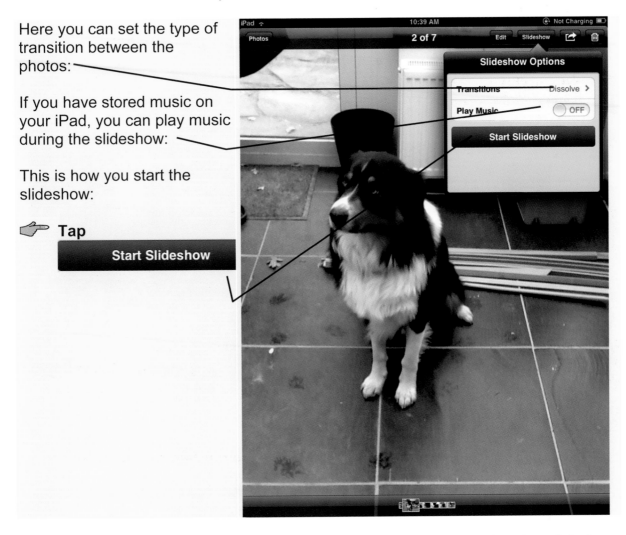

You will see the slideshow. If you have also made a video, this will be played during the slideshow. This is how you stop the slideshow:

☞ **Tap the screen**

The last photo that was displayed during the slideshow will freeze and remain on screen.

6.5 Sending a Photo by E-mail

If you have taken a nice picture and saved it on your iPad, you can share it by e-mail. Here is how to do that:

☞ **If necessary, open a photo** 𝄡⁷⁶

👉 **Tap the photo**

👉 **Tap**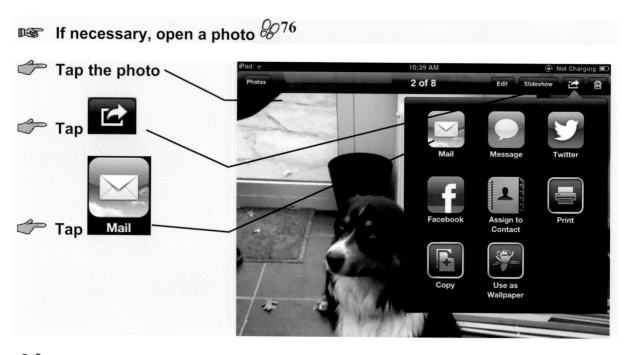

👉 **Tap** Mail

🩹 HELP! I cannot see the menu bar.
The menu bar will appear when you tap the photo.

A new message will be opened, which includes the photo:

You can send the message in the same way you learned in *Chapter 2 Sending E-mails with Your iPad*. For now, you do not need to do this:

👉 **Tap**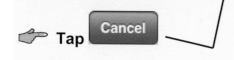

You will be asked if you want to save the draft:

☞ **Tap**

You will see the photo once again.

6.6 Printing a Photo

If you use a printer that supports the *AirPrint* function, you can print the photos on your iPad through a wireless connection.

 Tip

AirPrint
When this book was in the making, there were only a few printers (all Hewlett Packard printers) that supported the *AirPrint* option.

This is how you print a photo from your iPad:

☞ **If necessary, turn on Wi-Fi** 👣**10**

☞ **If necessary, tap the photo**

☞ **Tap**

☞ **Tap** **Print**

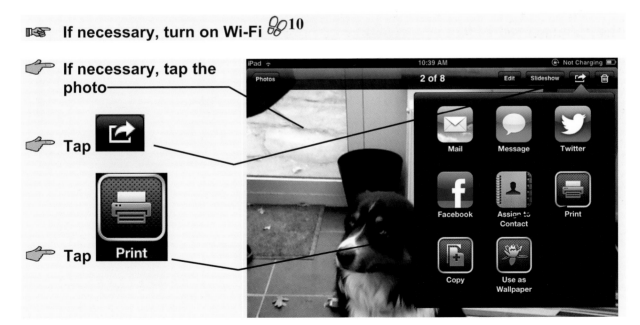

Select the right printer:

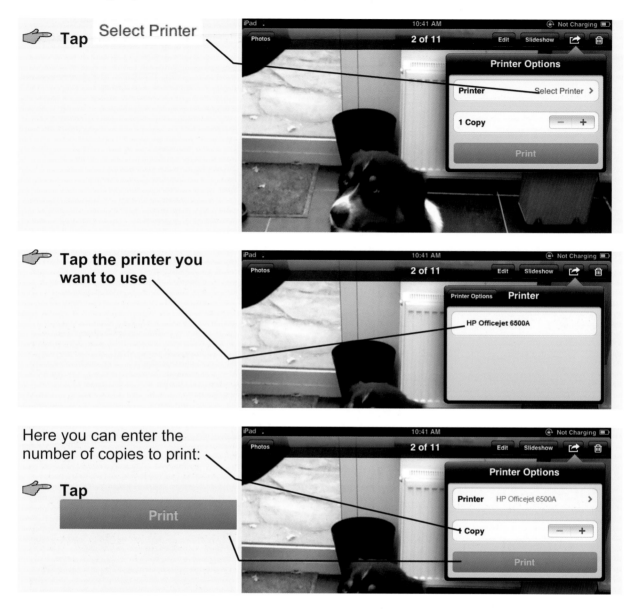

👉 **Tap** Select Printer

👉 **Tap the printer you want to use**

Here you can enter the number of copies to print:

👉 **Tap**

Print

The photo will be printed.

👉 **If necessary, turn off Wi-Fi** 👣⁷

👉 **Go back to the home screen** 👣⁸

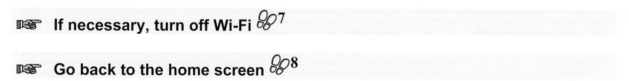

6.7 Copying Photos to the Computer

You can use *Windows Explorer* to copy the photos you have made with your iPad to your computer. This is how you do it:

☞ **Connect the iPad to the computer**

☞ **Close *iTunes*** $\mathcal{QQ}$66

☞ **If necessary, close the *AutoPlay* window** $\mathcal{QQ}$66

Open *Windows Explorer*:

Your iPad will be detected by *Windows*, as if it were a digital camera:

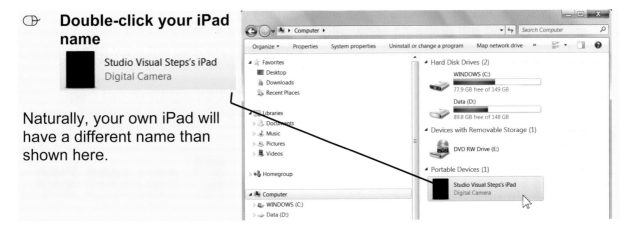

☞ **Tap**

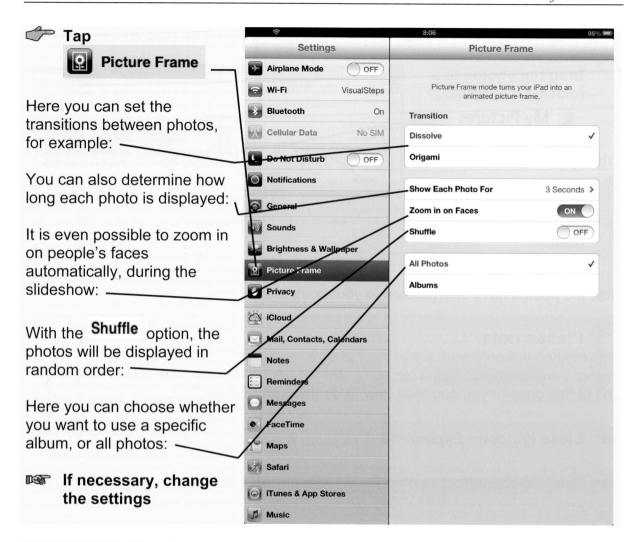

Picture Frame

Here you can set the
transitions between photos,
for example:

You can also determine how
long each photo is displayed:

It is even possible to zoom in
on people's faces
automatically, during the
slideshow:

With the **Shuffle** option, the
photos will be displayed in
random order:

Here you can choose whether
you want to use a specific
album, or all photos:

☞ **If necessary, change
the settings**

☞ **Go back to the home screen** ⚆⚆**8**

☞ **Put the iPad into sleep mode** ⚆⚆**1**

This is how you start the *Picture Frame* function:

☞ **Press the Home button**

6.10 Background Inform

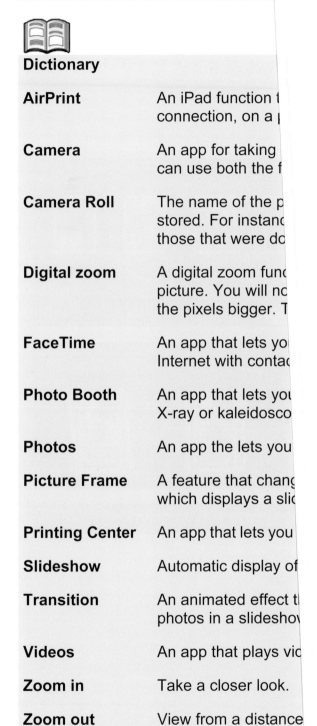

Dictionary

AirPrint	An iPad function t connection, on a
Camera	An app for taking can use both the f
Camera Roll	The name of the p stored. For instanc those that were dc
Digital zoom	A digital zoom func picture. You will nc the pixels bigger. T
FaceTime	An app that lets yo Internet with contac
Photo Booth	An app that lets you X-ray or kaleidosco
Photos	An app the lets you
Picture Frame	A feature that chang which displays a slic
Printing Center	An app that lets you
Slideshow	Automatic display of
Transition	An animated effect t photos in a slideshov
Videos	An app that plays vic
Zoom in	Take a closer look.
Zoom out	View from a distance

Source: iPad User Guide, Wikipedia

Do not unlock the iPad. Instead:

 **Tap**

The slideshow will be started. This is how you stop the slideshow:

 **Tap the screen**

Tap

☞ **If necessary, put the iPad into sleep mode or turn it off** 👣¹

You will see the Lock screen again.

In this chapter you have learned more about the *Camera, Photos* and *Photo Booth* apps. In the next few exercises, you can practice all the things you have learned.

☞ Start *Picture Frame*. ⚹⁸³

☞ Stop *Picture Frame*. ⚹⁸⁴

☞ If you want, put the iPad into

6.11 Tips

💡 Tip
Albums and photos
In the *Photos* app you can display your photos in various ways:

☞ **Open the *Photos* app** ⚹⁷⁵

☞ **If necessary, tap** Photos

In the *Photos* view you will see all the photos, below and next to each other:

In the *Albums* view the photos have been ordered and stacked:

In the *Places* view you will see a map showing the locations where the photos were taken:

If you tap a pin, you will see the set of photos that match this location.

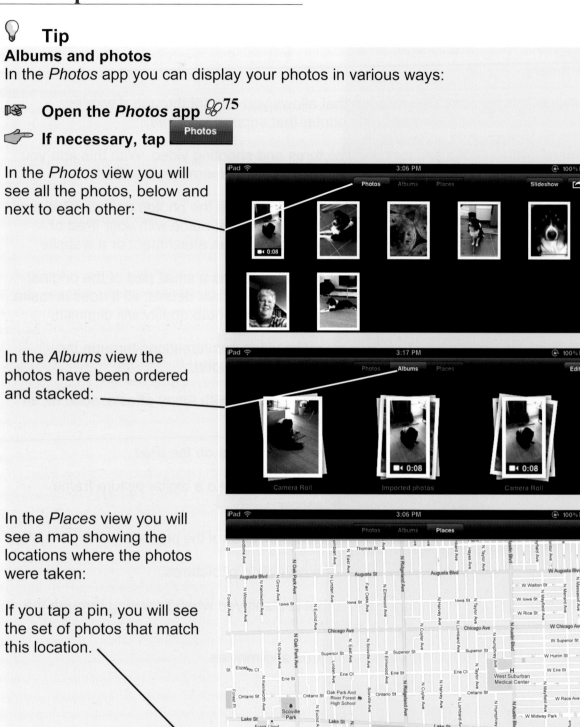

6.10 Background Information

Dictionary

AirPrint	An iPad function that allows you to print through a wireless connection, on a printer that supports *AirPrint*.
Camera	An app for taking pictures and shooting video. With this app you can use both the front and back cameras on the iPad.
Camera Roll	The name of the photo folder where the photos on your iPad are stored. For instance, the photos you made with your iPad or those that were downloaded from an attachment or a website.
Digital zoom	A digital zoom function that enlarges a small part of the original picture. You will not see any additional details; all it does is make the pixels bigger. That is why the photo quality will diminish.
FaceTime	An app that lets you make video conversations through the Internet with contacts all over the world.
Photo Booth	An app that lets you take pictures with funny effects, such as an X-ray or kaleidoscope photo.
Photos	An app the lets you view the photos on the iPad.
Picture Frame	A feature that changes your iPad into a digital picture frame which displays a slideshow.
Printing Center	An app that lets you view the status of the printer and the print jobs.
Slideshow	Automatic display of a collection of pictures.
Transition	An animated effect that is displayed when browsing through the photos in a slideshow.
Videos	An app that plays videos and movies.
Zoom in	Take a closer look.
Zoom out	View from a distance.

Source: iPad User Guide, Wikipedia

6.11 Tips

 Tip

Albums and photos

In the *Photos* app you can display your photos in various ways:

 Open the *Photos* app ⁷⁵

☞ **If necessary, tap** Photos

In the *Photos* view you will
see all the photos, below and
next to each other:

In the *Albums* view the
photos have been ordered
and stacked:

In the *Places* view you will
see a map showing the
locations where the photos
were taken:

If you tap a pin, you will see
the set of photos that match
this location.

Tip

Use photo as wallpaper
You can also use your own photo as a background for the lock screen or the home screen. This is how to do that:

☞ **Tap**

☞ **Tap**

Now you can choose whether you want to use this photo as wallpaper for the lock screen, the home screen, or both:

☞ **Tap**

 Tip

Copy photos and video to your iPad through iTunes
Your iPad is a useful tool for showing your favorite pictures and videos to others. Actually, you can also use the photos on your computer. This is done by synchronizing the folder containing the photos and videos with your iPad, through *iTunes*.

☞ **Connect your iPad to the computer**

The *iTunes* will automatically open:

⊕ **By** DEVICES **, click your iPad, for example** 🔲 Studio Visual S...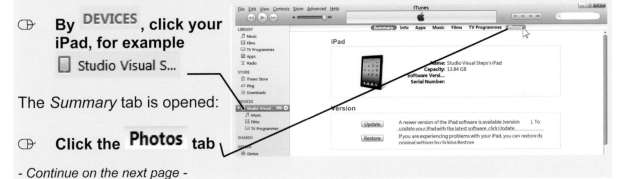

The *Summary* tab is opened:

⊕ **Click the** Photos **tab**

- Continue on the next page -

In this example, the photos from the (*My*) *Pictures* folder will be synchronized:

 Check the box ☑ **by**
Sync Photos from

The My Pictures ⬍
folder has already been
selected: ——

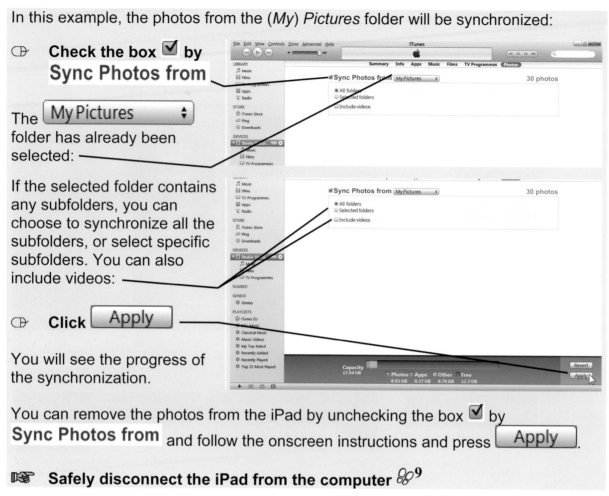

If the selected folder contains
any subfolders, you can
choose to synchronize all the
subfolders, or select specific
subfolders. You can also
include videos: ——

 Click Apply

You will see the progress of
the synchronization.

You can remove the photos from the iPad by unchecking the box ☑ by
Sync Photos from and follow the onscreen instructions and press Apply .

☞ **Safely disconnect the iPad from the computer** 👣⁹

💡 **Tip**

Directly transfer photos to your iPad with the Camera Connection Kit
A very useful accessory to your iPad is the *Camera Connection Kit*. This is a set of
two connectors that lets you quickly and easily transfer photos from your digital
camera to your iPad. You can buy this *Camera Connection Kit* for about $29 (as of
October 2012) at your *Apple* store.

💡 **Tip**

Assign a photo to a contact
If you have taken a nice picture of one of your contacts, you can assign this picture to
his or her contact information.

👉 **Tap**

- Continue on the next page -

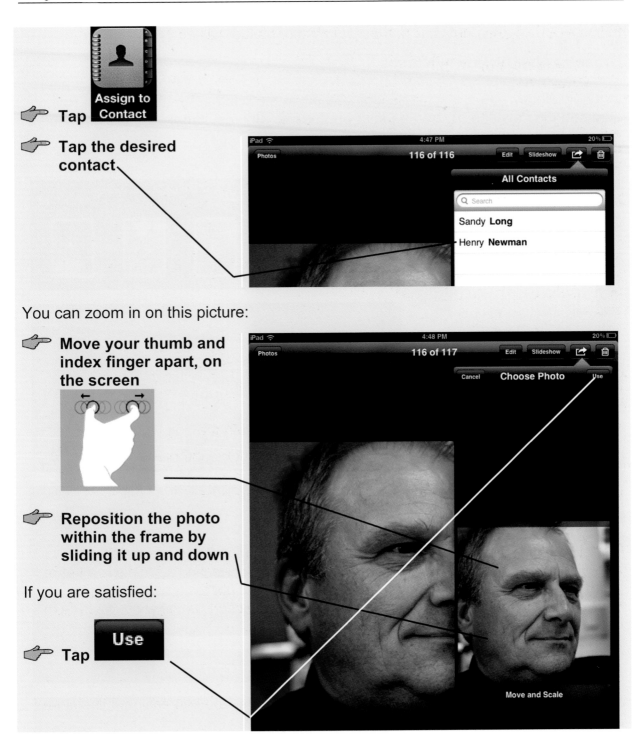

☞ Tap **Assign to Contact**

☞ Tap the desired contact.

You can zoom in on this picture:

☞ **Move your thumb and index finger apart, on the screen**

☞ **Reposition the photo within the frame by sliding it up and down**

If you are satisfied:

☞ Tap **Use**

💡 **Tip**

The Videos app
With the *Videos* app you can't shoot videos or playback your own videos. This app allows you to buy or rent movies from the *iTunes Store*.

💡 Tip

Organize your photos in albums

You can create albums for your photos directly on your iPad. When you add a photo to a new album, you are actually adding a link to the photo from the Camera Roll album to the new one. By sorting your photos into albums, it makes it easier to find a series of photos about a specific subject later on.

You can create a new album like this:

☞ Tap **Albums**

You will see the albums on your iPad. In this example, you only see the Camera Roll album. This album contains all the photos you have made with your iPad.

☞ Tap **Edit**

☞ Tap **+**

⌨ Type a name

☞ Tap **Save**

☞ Tap the desired photos

☞ Tap **Done**

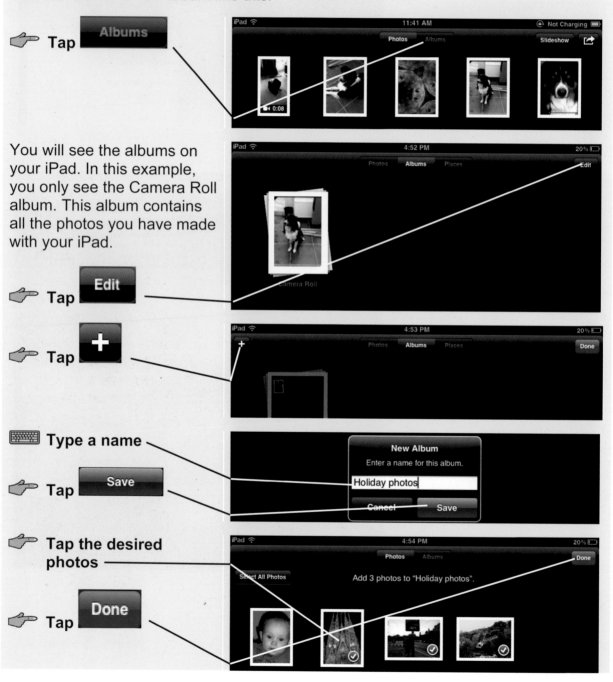

Tip

Photo editing

There are some basic photo editing options available in the *Photos* app. You can use the features to rotate, enhance, crop or remove red-eye.

☞ **Open a photo**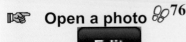

👉 **Tap**

In the bottom of the screen you can see the various options:

You can give one a try, for instance the rotate feature. You can always go back to the photo in its original state by tapping the

Revert to Original in the top of your screen.

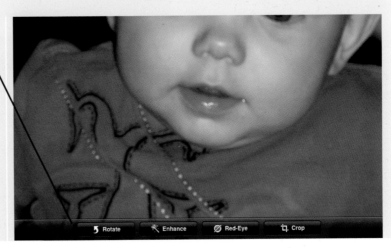

 Tip

Video playback

If you have shoot a video or transferred videos to your iPad (see page 251), you can view them via the Camera Roll in the *Camera* app. You can also open a video with the *Photos* app. You need to navigate to the Camera Roll. There you will see your videos in between your photos. In this example, a video of a lama will be viewed using the *Camera* app.

You can open the video like this:

In the bottom of your screen:

👉 **Tap**

- Continue on the next page -

You will see your video. To play the video:

👉 **Tap**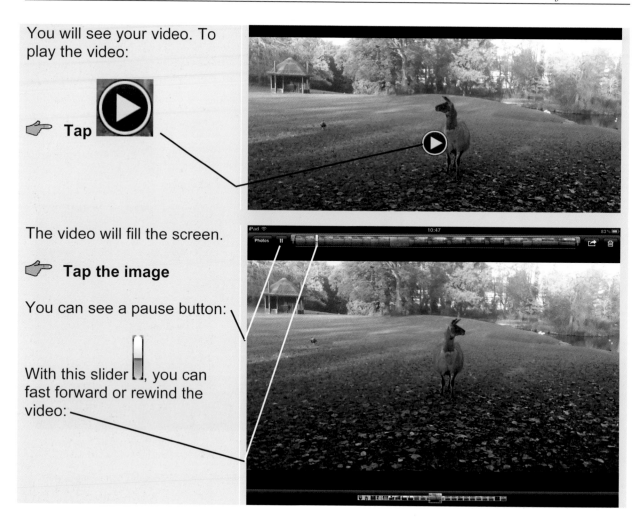

The video will fill the screen.

👉 **Tap the image**

You can see a pause button:

With this slider , you can fast forward or rewind the video:

💡 **Tip**

Make video calls with FaceTime
You can use the *FaceTime* app to make video calls with the iPad. To use *FaceTime* you will need an Internet connection and an *Apple ID*. If you do not have one yet, you can read how to create an *Apple ID* in *Chapter 5 Downloading Apps*.

👉 **If necessary, turn on Wi-Fi** 👣¹⁰

👉 **Tap**

- Continue on the next page -

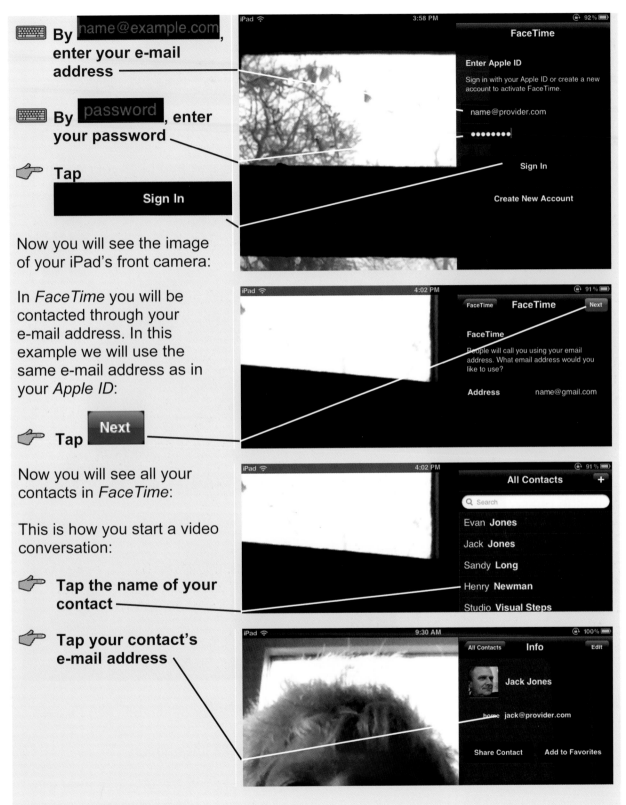

By name@example.com, enter your e-mail address ————

By password, enter your password

☞ Tap

Sign In

Now you will see the image of your iPad's front camera:

In *FaceTime* you will be contacted through your e-mail address. In this example we will use the same e-mail address as in your *Apple ID*:

☞ Tap Next

Now you will see all your contacts in *FaceTime*:

This is how you start a video conversation:

☞ **Tap the name of your contact** ———

☞ **Tap your contact's e-mail address**

- Continue on the next page -

The iPad will try to make a connection. You will hear the phone ring:

Please note: The contact needs to be online, and needs to have added your name and e-mail address to his or her contacts.
Once the connection has been made, you will be able to see and hear your contact:

In this way you can hold a video conversation with contacts all over the world.

Use the button to mute the sound of your microphone:

If you want to end the conversation:

☞ **Tap** **Stop**

With the button you can use the camera on the back of the iPad.

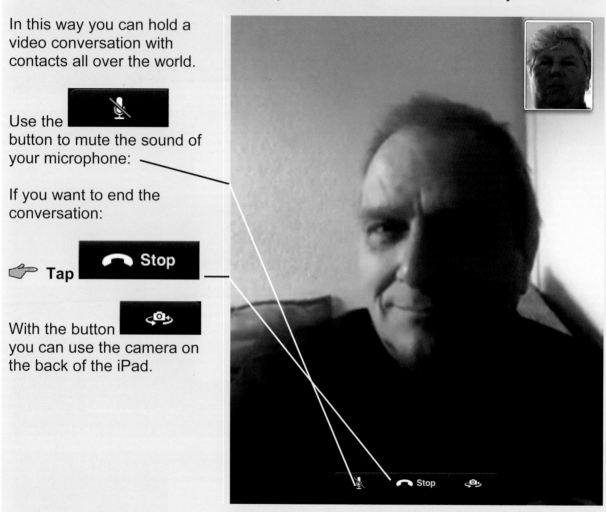

Tip: you can also open the *FaceTime* app from within the *Contacts* app. Simply tap the FaceTime button that you see by the your contact's information.

It is also possible to make video calls using the Skype app. You can call or chat with other *Skype* users. You can download this free app from the *App Store*.

7. Music

Your iPad is equipped with an extensive music player, the *Music* app. If you have stored any music files on your computer, you can transfer this music to your iPad, through *iTunes*. In the *iTunes Store* you can also purchase songs or entire albums.

In this chapter you will learn how to:

- add music to the *iTunes Library*;
- synchronize music with your iPad;
- buy music on your iPad;
- play music on your iPad.

7.1 Adding Music to iTunes

Your iPad comes with a very extensive music player, called the *Music* app. If you have stored any music files on your computer, you can use *iTunes* to transfer these files to your iPad.

☞ **Open *iTunes* on your computer** 🦶100

You will see the *iTunes* window. This is how you add the folder containing the music files to the *Library*:

☞ **Click** File

☞ **Click**
Add Folder to Library.

If you want to add a single file, or multiple files, select
Add File to Library...

In this example we have used the folder containing the sample files that come with *Windows*, but you can use your own music files if you want:

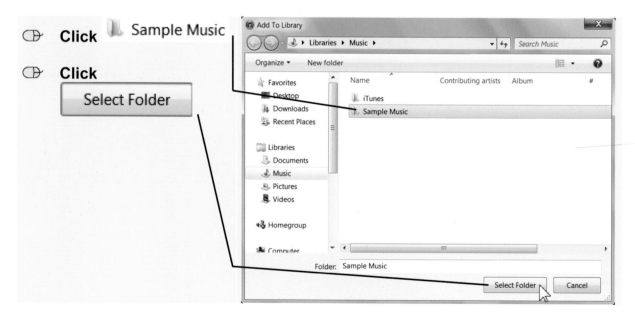

☞ **Click** 🎵 Sample Music

☞ **Click**
Select Folder

After a while, these songs will appear in your *iTunes* program:

7.2 Synchronizing Music with Your iPad

Once the songs have been transferred to *iTunes*, it is very simple to add them to your iPad.

☞ **Connect your iPad to the computer**

The iPad will be displayed in *iTunes*. Select the songs you want to transfer:

Click the first song

Press and hold it down
⇧ Shift

Click the last song

Release
⇧ Shift

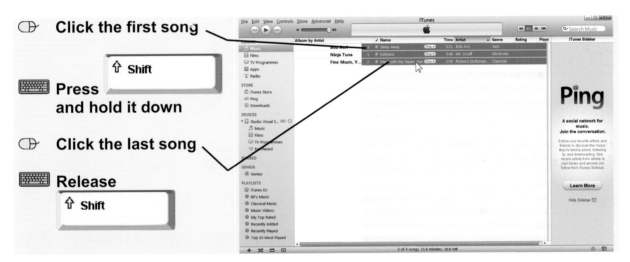

The songs have been selected. Now you can copy the songs to your iPad:

Drag the selected songs to
📱 Studio Visual S...

The mouse pointer will turn

into   :

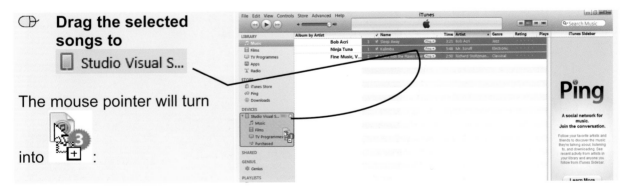

You will see a progress bar indicating the progress of the update:

View the contents of the iPad:

☞ **By** ⬜ Studio Visual S..., **click** 🎵 Music

You will see that the songs have been copied to your iPad:

Now you can disconnect the iPad and close *iTunes*:

☞ **Safely disconnect the iPad** 👣⁹ **and close *iTunes*** 👣⁶⁶

7.3 Buying Music on Your iPad

You can also add music files to your iPad right away, by purchasing songs in the *iTunes Store*.

☞ **If necessary, wake the iPad up or turn it on** 👣²

☞ **If necessary, turn on Wi-Fi** 👣¹⁰

This is how you open the *iTunes* app:

☞ **Tap** **iTunes**

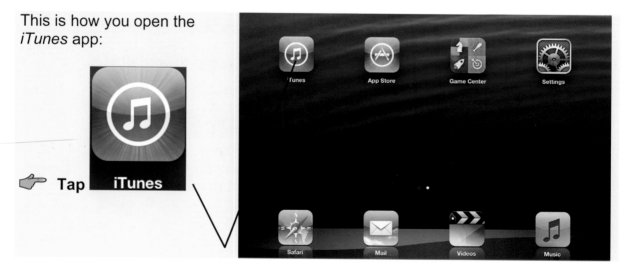

You will see the home page for the *iTunes Store*:

You can see the latest trends by going to the top charts:

 Tap Charts

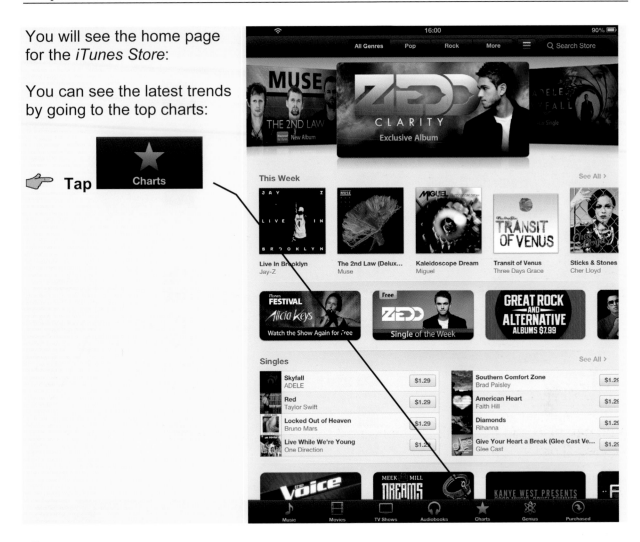

Tip
Search

You can use the search box Q Search Store and search directly for your favorite artist or song.

 Please note:

The appearance of a web page by a web store, including the *iTunes Store*, will often change. The *iTunes Store* is actually a website that is opened on your iPad.
The screen that you see will very likely be different from the screen shots you see in this book.

You will see the Top 14 top-selling songs and albums:

The top charts on your own screen will look different.

You can view more items:

☞ **Swipe upwards over the list**

To go back to the first six numbers:

☞ **Swipe downwards over the list**

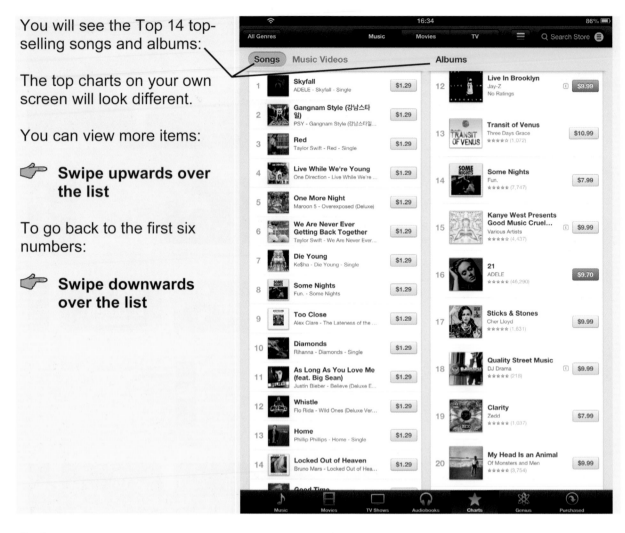

Before you decide to purchase a song, you can listen to a thirty second fragment of the song. Just give it a try:

☞ **Tap a song**

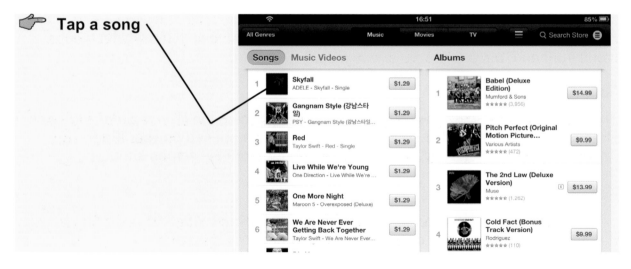

A new window pops open and you will see the album that contains this song. This is how you can listen to the fragment:

 Tap the song title ——

The fragment will be played.

If there are more numbers on the album, you can listen to a few more songs.

This is how you return to the top charts:

 Tap your screen anywhere outside of the popup window

The popup will close.

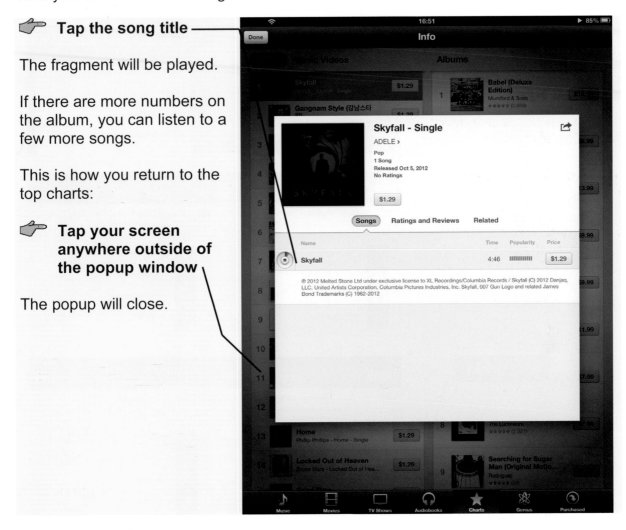

If you want to buy a song, you can use the same method as for buying an app, as explained in *Chapter 5 Downloading Apps*. You can also use your prepaid *iTunes* credit from an *iTunes Gift Card* to buy music.

☜ Please note:

To follow the examples in the next section, you need to have an *Apple ID*. You also need to have some prepaid credit or you need to have a credit card linked to your *Apple ID*. For more information, read *Chapter 5 Downloading Apps*.

☜ Please note:

In the following example, we will actually purchase a song, which will cost $1.29. Follow these steps literally, only if you really want to buy this song.

You are going to search for a song:

👉 **Tap**

🔍 Search Store

👉 **Type the name of an artist**

👉 **Tap the artist**

👉 **Tap the price next to the song you want to purchase** ——

In this example, a song costs **$1.29** . But these prices may be subject to change.

👉 **Tap** **BUY SONG**

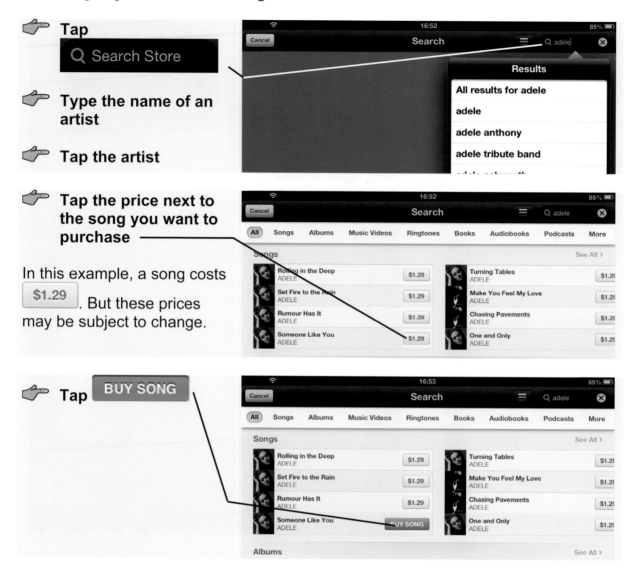

If you are still logged on with your *Apple ID* you only need to enter your password:

⌨ **Type your password**

👉 **Tap** **OK**

If you had signed off, you will see this screen:

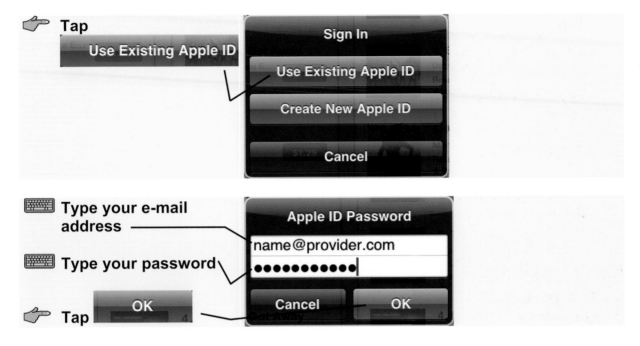

Tap
Use Existing Apple ID

Type your e-mail address

Type your password

Tap OK

The song will be downloaded:

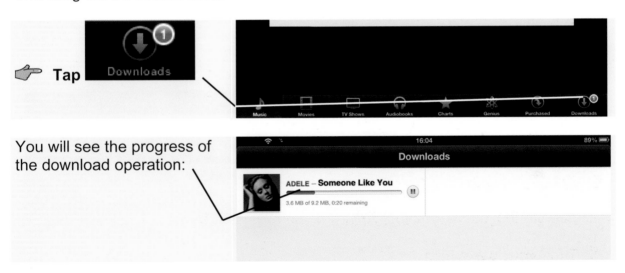

Tap Downloads

You will see the progress of the download operation:

After the song has been downloaded, you can view your purchases in the *Music* app:

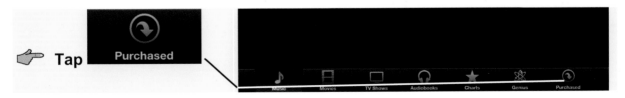

Tap Purchased

You will see your purchases:

☞ **Tap the artist**

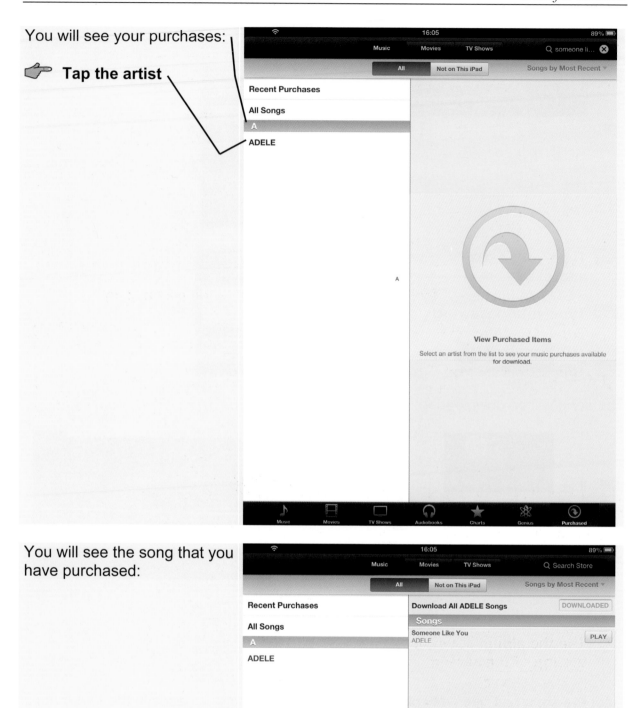

You will see the song that you have purchased:

☞ **Go back to the home screen** 👣⁸

7.4 Playing Music with the Music App

This is how you open the *Music* app:

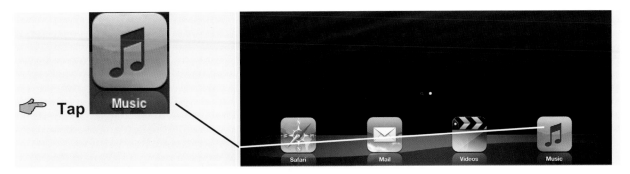

☞ **Tap**

You will all see the songs again on your iPad. This is how you play a song:

☞ **Tap a song title, for instance,**
   Someone Like You

The song will be played and the album cover will be displayed on a full screen:

If the image on your screen is not displayed in full screen mode:

☞ **Tap the album cover at the top of the screen**

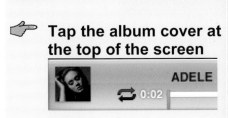

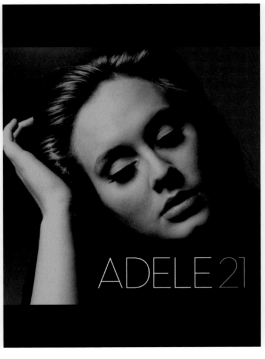

☞ **Tap the image**

You will see various buttons to control and adjust the playback of the music:

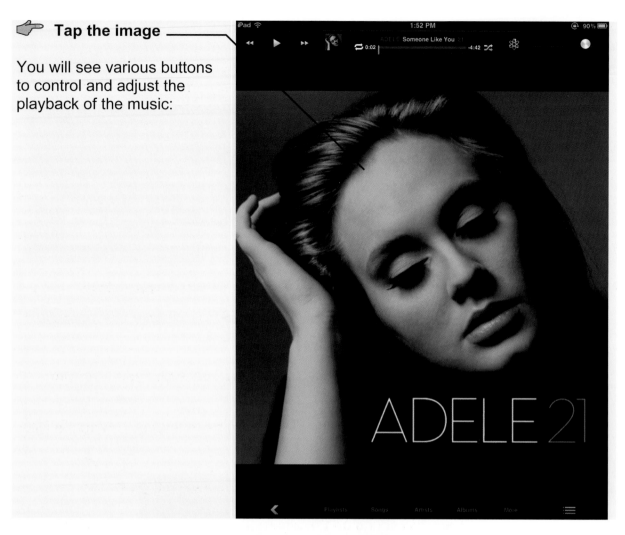

The bar with all the control buttons for playing music looks like this:

This is how all the buttons work:

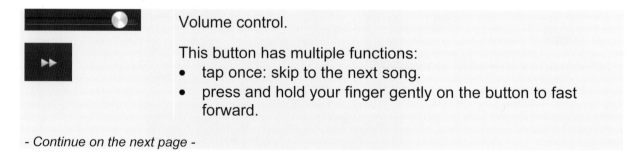

Volume control.

This button has multiple functions:
- tap once: skip to the next song.
- press and hold your finger gently on the button to fast forward.

- Continue on the next page -

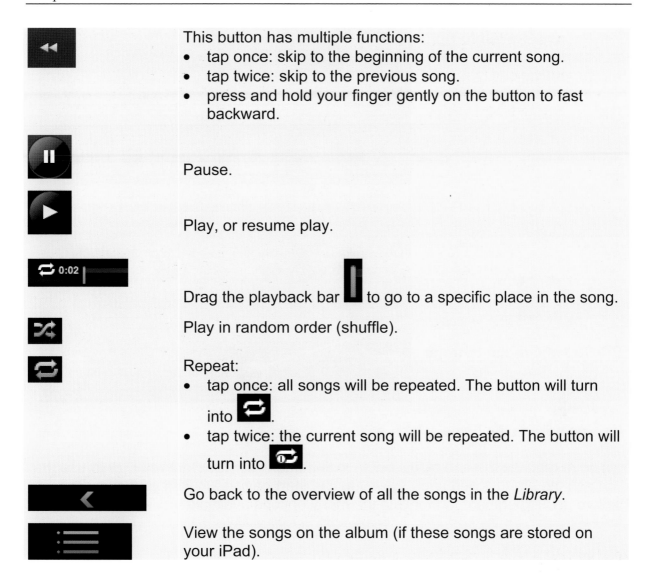

This button has multiple functions:
- tap once: skip to the beginning of the current song.
- tap twice: skip to the previous song.
- press and hold your finger gently on the button to fast backward.

Pause.

Play, or resume play.

Drag the playback bar to go to a specific place in the song.

Play in random order (shuffle).

Repeat:
- tap once: all songs will be repeated. The button will turn into .
- tap twice: the current song will be repeated. The button will turn into .

Go back to the overview of all the songs in the *Library*.

View the songs on the album (if these songs are stored on your iPad).

During playback, you can quit the *Music* app and do something else:

☞ **Go back to the home screen** $\mathcal{O}\!\mathcal{O}^8$

The music is still being played. You can display the *Music* app control buttons in any of the other apps:

☞ **Open the recently used apps** $\mathcal{O}\!\mathcal{O}^{42}$

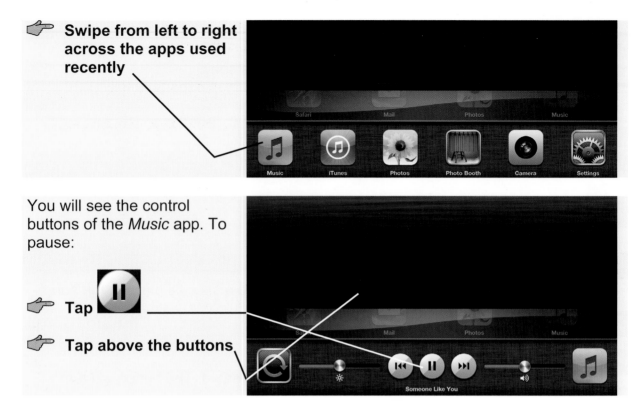

Swipe from left to right across the apps used recently

You will see the control buttons of the *Music* app. To pause:

☞ **Tap** ❚❚

☞ **Tap above the buttons**

Now you will see the home screen again.

You have reached the end of this book. In this book you have learned how to use the iPad and the pre-installed apps. Now you can start having fun with your own iPad. Explore and experiment further with the many options available.

7.5 Visual Steps

By now you will have noticed that the Visual Steps method is the quickest and most efficient way to learn more about computing and software. All books published by Visual Steps use this same method. In various series, we have published a large number of books on a wide variety of topics, including *Windows*, *Mac, iPad* and *iPhone,* photo editing, video editing, (free) software programs such as *Picasa* and many other topics.

On the **www.visualsteps.com** website you can click the Catalog page to find an overview of all the Visual Steps titles, including an extensive description. Each title allows you to preview the full table of contents and a sample chapter in a PDF format. In this way, you can quickly determine if a specific title will meet your expectations. All titles can be ordered online and are also available in bookstores across the USA, Canada, United Kingdom, Australia and New Zealand.

Furthermore, this website offers these extras, among other things:

- free computer guides and booklets (PDF files) on all sorts of subjects;
- frequently asked questions and their answers;
- information on the free Computer Certificate that you can acquire at the certificate's website www.ccforseniors.com;
- a free notify-me service: receive an e-mail as soon as a new book is published.

7.6 Exercises

To be able to quickly apply the things you have learned, you can work through these exercises. Have you forgotten how to do something? Use the numbers next to the footsteps 🐾¹ to look up the item in the appendix *How Do I Do That Again?*

Exercise 1: Listen to Music

In this exercise you are going to listen to the music on your iPad.

☞ If necessary, wake the iPad up from sleep mode or turn it on. 🐾²

☞ Open the *Music* app. 🐾**101**

☞ Play the first song. 🐾**102**

If the album cover is not displayed in full screen mode:

☞ Tap the album cover at the top of the screen.

☞ Turn up the volume. 🐾**103**

☞ Skip to the next song. 🐾**104**

☞ Repeat the current song. 🐾**105**

☞ Disable the repeat function. 🐾**106**

☞ Enable the shuffle/random playback function. 🐾**107**

☞ Skip to the next song. 🐾**104**

☞ Disable the shuffle/random playback function. 🐾**108**

☞ Go back to the *Library*. 🐾**109**

☞ Pause playback. 🐾**110**

☞ Go back to the home screen. 🐾**8**

☞ If you want, put the iPad into sleep mode or turn it off. 🐾¹

7.7 Background Information

Dictionary

Apple ID   A combination of a user name and a password. You need an
                      Apple ID to use *FaceTime* and to purchase and/or download
                      music from the *iTunes Store* or apps from the *App Store*.

Music   An app that plays music.

Playlist   A collection of songs, ordered in a certain way.

Source: User Guide iPad

7.8 Tips

 Tip

Transfer purchased Music to iTunes
In *iTunes* you can transfer your purchases to your computer. This way, you will have
a backup copy of the music you purchased and you will also be able to synchronize
them with other devices, such as an iPhone. To do this you can use the tip *Transfer
purchases to iTunes* from *Chapter 5 Downloading Apps*. Transferring music works
similar to transferring apps.

 Tip

Create a playlist
Another useful function in the *Music* app is the option for creating playlists. In a
playlist, you can collect and sort your favorite songs, any way you want. When you
are done, you can play this list over and over again. Here is how to create a new
playlist in the *Music* app:

In the bottom of the screen:

- Continue on the next page -

If you recently bought music in the *iTunes Store* you might see this screen:

👉 **Tap** Playlists

In the top of the screen:

👉 **Tap** New

Enter a name for the new playlist:

⌨️ **Type a name, for example:** Favorite songs

👉 **Tap** Save

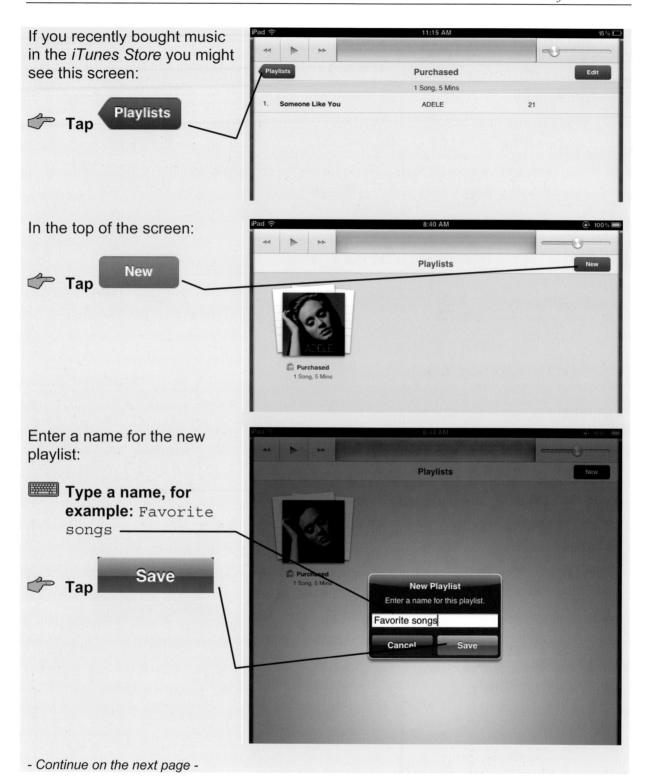

- Continue on the next page -

Now you can add songs to the playlist:

☞ **Select the songs you want to add to your playlist and tap ⊕ next to these songs**

☞ **Tap** Done

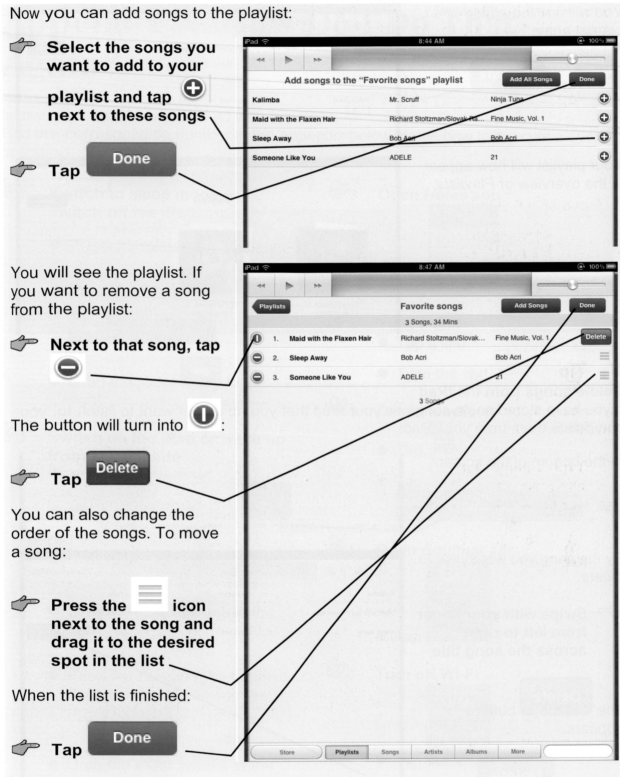

You will see the playlist. If you want to remove a song from the playlist:

☞ **Next to that song, tap ⊖**

The button will turn into ⊘ :

☞ **Tap** Delete

You can also change the order of the songs. To move a song:

☞ **Press the ≡ icon next to the song and drag it to the desired spot in the list**

When the list is finished:

☞ **Tap** Done

- Continue on the next page -

Appendix B. Download and Install iTunes

In this appendix you can read how to download and install *iTunes*. *iTunes* can be downloaded (for free) from the *Apple* website, the manufacturers of the iPad and *iTunes*.

 Please note:

The first step is to download the *iTunes* program. You will find this program on the *Apple* website.

☞ **Surf to www.apple.com/itunes/download** 🕮*111*

You may need to install the *QuickTime* plug-in first, before you can download *iTunes*. If you do not see the window below, you can skip this step:

☞ **Click**

   Always run on this site

Apple will ask if you want to sign up for product news and special offers. But you do not need to enter your e-mail address to download *iTunes*:

☞ **Uncheck the boxes ☑ by**
   Email me New On iTunes and sp
   iTunes offers.
   and
   Keep me up to date with Apple
   software updates, and the late:
   information on products and se

☞ **Click**

   Download Now ⊙

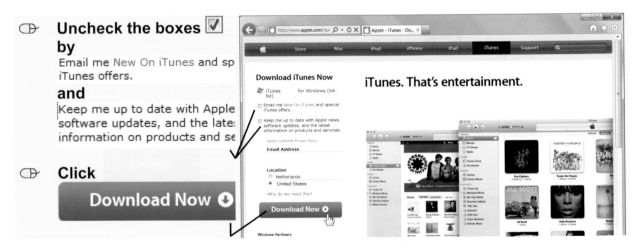

In the bottom of the window, a security warning will probably appear:

⏁ **Click** [<u>R</u>un]

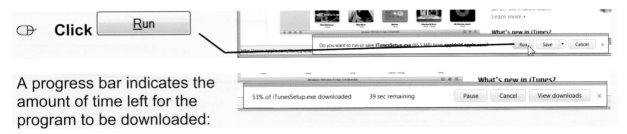

A progress bar indicates the amount of time left for the program to be downloaded:

In a few moments, you will see the installation window with information about *iTunes*:

⏁ **Click** [Next >]

In the next window you can select the installation options for *iTunes*:

In this example, *iTunes* is the default player for playing audio files. The software will be automatically updated. If you do not want this, you can uncheck the boxes:

You can also change the language, if you want:

⏁ **Click** [🛡 Install]

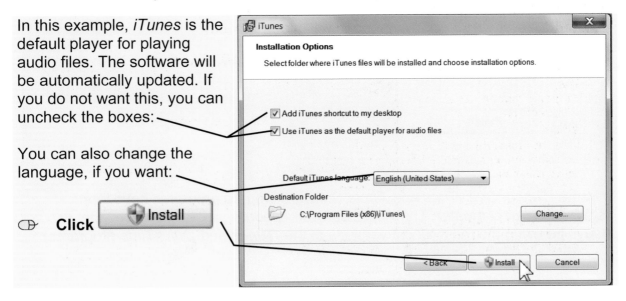

If you are using *Windows 7* or *Windows Vista*, your screen may now turn dark. You will be asked for permission to continue with the installation.

Now the *iTunes* program will be installed and if needed, the *QuickTime* program also. *QuickTime* is the multimedia platform from the *Apple* Corporation; you will need this program if you want to use *iTunes*. This may take several minutes. You will see the progress of the installation process in the window.
If you are using *Windows 7* or *Windows Vista*, your screen may turn dark once again. You will be asked for permission to continue with the installation:

The installation process continues:

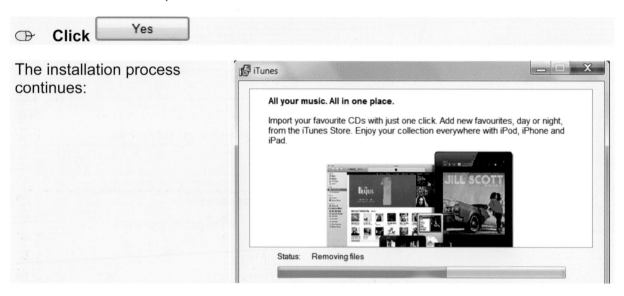

After the installation has finished, you do not need to open *iTunes* right away:

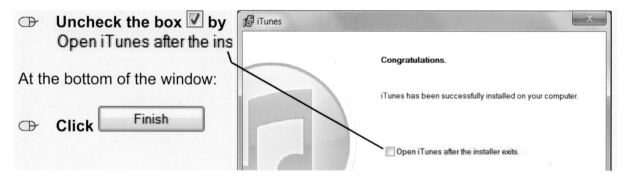

⊕ **Uncheck the box** ☑ **by Open iTunes after the ins**

At the bottom of the window:

⊕ **Click** [Finish]

Now the *iTunes*, *QuickTime* and *Apple Software Update* programs have been installed to your computer. The *Apple Software Update* program ensures that you will always be using the most recent versions of the *iTunes* and *QuickTime* programs.

☞ **Close** *Internet Explorer* 𝒪𝒪**66**

Appendix C. Index

Creating a Photo Book for SENIORS

Creating a Photo Book for SENIORS
Everything you need to create a professionally printed photo book

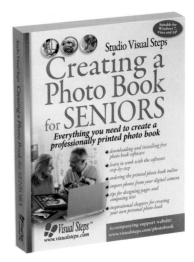

Author: Studio Visual Steps
ISBN 978 90 5905 247 5
Book type: Paperback
Nr of pages: 240 pages
Accompanying website:
www.visualsteps.com/photobook

Creating your own photo book of memories has never been easier! ***Creating a Photo Book for SENIORS*** will give you easy to understand step-by-step instructions with clear illustrations to guide you through the entire process.
Using free photo book software, this book will show you how to lay out your story with text, photos and other graphical elements. This book offers lots of original ideas and practical tips for composing your text. For instance, the story of your childhood, your son or daughter's wedding, your family history, a travelogue, a chronicle of a baby's first year, even your own autobiography.
You will also learn how to transfer photos from your digital camera to your computer and incorporate them into your book and how to scan photos or other historical documents so that you can use them to further embellish your special photo book.
And, finally, take advantage of the printing services offered by the photo book provider to insure that you will get a beautifully-crafted and professionally-bound photo book at the end of the process.
Making a photo book has never been so easy!

You will learn how to:
- download and install the photo book software
- work with photo book software
- get your photo book printed
- transfer photos from a camera to the PC, scan photos
- use practical and creative tips for writing and layout
- view inspirational chapters to help you compile your own photo book